D0881303

# 63 Innovation Nuggets
## (for aspiring innovators)

George E. L. Barbee

First edition

Library of Congress Control Number: 2015951880


ISBN-10:
ISBN-13: 978-0-9967531-0-4

*To my wife, Molly, my family, and
many business colleagues.*

# Contents

## Acknowledgements

Innovation is not an "I" thing but a "WE" thing.

In summary, I am grateful for PricewaterhouseCoopers, hundreds of collegial partners, and many clients whom I have worked with globally in close, trusting relationships including General Electric, PepsiCo, and Gillette as well as IBM and Procter & Gamble. I am also grateful to my entrepreneurial colleagues at the Consumer Financial Institute (CFI) and the Victory Van Board.

Also deserving of recognition and thanks are my colleagues at the University of Virginia Darden School of Business, including six deans, a distinguished faculty, and hundreds of my MBA and executive students. Many brilliant colleagues and authors also supported me in class sessions including Jim Gilmore (*The Experience Economy*), Shanker Ramamurthy (IBM senior executive), Alec Horniman, Robert Spekman, and others.

Additionally, I celebrate the many authors who have inspired my innovative thinking over the years and my freelance book editor, Susan Carlson, who has taught me how to use technology to "Be There ... Without Really Being There" (page 32) and who was *there* for every step along the way to publish this book.

The greatest support of all comes from my wife, Molly, who has been a pillar for nearly 40 years—and the love shared for our family of four boys during my way-too-extensive travels.

A complete list of credits including the people, publications, and companies who have inspired me can be found on pages 139-143. You can also learn more about my work in innovation in the *Epilogue* and *About the Author* sections at the end of this book.

# Preface

## What's In It For You?

I was inspired to write this book for three primary reasons:

- Most of us can be more innovative in business than we give ourselves credit for—especially when we realize *innovation* is a lot broader than just *invention.*
- We can quickly learn to more innovatively *observe* and then *transfer* these innovations from one category to another.
- Being more innovative is, in fact, *learnable* and even self-teachable.

I've been fortunate to observe and learn this during 45 years of practical, innovative business experiences across 40 countries and across Fortune 100 companies. Across smaller and entrepreneurial companies. And in the most recent 15 years, teaching MBA students and executives at the University of Virginia Darden School of Business. Along the way, we were most fortunate to have some national media attention, which has been further reinforcing.

## The Book's Organization

There are four different categories, or clusters, of nuggets in this book that can help you reflect and become more innovative:

In the **Innovative Strategies** section, there are practical insights related to strategies for innovative success in the marketplace.

The **Innovative Observations** section can help us better see what innovation is around us already. For some, this will be a broader definition as to what business innovation really is.

The **Organizational Effectiveness** section focuses on how to improve an organization's ability to accomplish innovative goals.

And finally, the **Personal Strategies** section includes tips and insights related to one's personal life. What can you do to foster and improve your creative thinking and innovation?

Any one nugget by itself may not shake the earth, but I believe you will find that they all add up—like a collection of panned nuggets that take on significant value in their totality. Perhaps one nugget is timely, or when juxtaposed with another, it takes on greater meaning for you. Each of these nuggets are supported by anecdotes—war stories, if you will, that bring the concepts to life.

This is a *Think Book*.

It is not intended to be read from start to finish. Instead, peruse the sections that grab your attention first. Focus on one page at a time, and let the ideas settle in. Pause and reflect.

You'll notice that there is a lot of white space on the nugget pages. Make notes if you'd like. *Make them your own*. Bounce around. Sometimes reordering on your own will help you make a connection someone else might not have made.

I have continued to use these nuggets to coach hundreds of executives to help them grow their businesses through innovation. They are not hard and fast rules. They are reflections. But they have worked for me, personally, and for those I have had the pleasure of working with around the world.

Let me know what resonates for you and your own story and progress. Find me online through my website (www.InnovationNuggets.com) and let's have a conversation.

# 63 Innovation Nuggets
(for aspiring innovators)

George E. L. Barbee

© 2015

# Innovative Strategies

# 1. Leading Innovation With Vision

Innovation is best led by vision—not by tight management or with a big stick: *"We have to do it, or else."*

Successful innovators can paint a picture of the future. What need is being filled? How can the product or service fill it uniquely?

Or, what possible new opportunity exists out there that has not yet been identified? Perhaps a development or new technology in one area opens up an opportunity in another?

People like to be associated with a winner. A winning concept. A winning team. A long-term success.

Achieving buy-in to the desired end game is key. It will keep the team positively focused and sustain the team during the inevitable disappointments and trying times.

In a global economy with its inherent complexities, innovative decision-making needs to happen at lower levels in the organization and in concert with senior management's leadership and vision.

Innovation is best led by vision.

Encourage it.

Develop it.

Reward it.

## Anecdote: Leading Innovation With Vision

General Electric, under the leadership of Jack Welch, coined a new word, "boundarylessness," to describe a common problem: siloed behavior by function, division, or country. In a way, the difficult pronunciation of "boundarylessness" brought attention to its importance.

GE had been financially measured by division for years, but unfortunately, it bred siloed behavior and lack of cooperation. After a few exciting experiments across multi-divisional wins in GE Aviation, GE Healthcare, GE Plastics, GE Appliances and Lighting, and GE Capital, there was good reason to change. It meant winning more business going forward.

Welch began celebrating "across boundary" wins through his internal communications, the Annual Report, and across a barrage of national and international media PR. Even though the organization had not quite arrived at its goals, he celebrated its successes—and the vision of being there.

I vividly recall the celebration and raising up of David Calhoun, an executive who had risen through the GE ranks. He was in charge of Internal Audit, Locomotives, and transferred to a new frontier in Singapore which opened up Asia.

Calhoun was celebrated for his "boundarylessness" attitude and actions while working across divisions, functions, and countries within GE. He was an executive to watch for a successful career.

Having a vision is an important start, but reinforcing that vision with success stories and celebrating it with individuals can make it come alive in implementation.

Large and small companies alike have the need to lead by vision. Not only across functions or across divisions but also across processes, countries, and even customers.

## 2. Piloting at 30,000 Feet. Piloting at Ground Level.

We're all familiar with the concept of seeing a situation or problem from 30,000 feet above—of grasping the "big picture" or seeing something from "the top down."

We're also likely familiar with seeing a situation at ground level: mired in the details and unable to "see the forest through the trees."

A successful innovator is often able to do both.

A successful innovator is a visionary—strategic and able to rise up to the "big picture" at 30,000 feet.

A successful innovator is also able to execute—to get down and dirty, make things happen, and bring about action. To be just a few feet away and examine things closely.

Successful innovation takes both. Ideally, you should have these abilities within yourself, but if not, be able to attract the skills around you.

A successful pilot needs skills at high altitude and at ground level.

## Anecdote: Piloting at 30,000 Feet. Piloting at Ground Level.

Several years prior to 1998, when Price Waterhouse (PW) merged with Coopers & Lybrand to form PricewaterhouseCoopers (PwC), several of us evolved a vision that we could organize differently around our *non-audit* clients to grow the firm faster than we could by relying on our current audit clients.

Further analysis showed that we were doing some type of work for 350 of the Fortune 500 somewhere in the world—in addition to the 100 audit clients already celebrated in Price Waterhouse's literature and PR.

This was the vision from 30,000 feet above: organize around the non-audit clients.

Armed with this vision, we then had to work out a plan at the ground level. We picked three Fortune 500 companies and decided to focus on them globally: GE, PepsiCo, and Gillette. This became my focus, and I needed to assemble teams.

We identified executives in each company with whom we had a relationship and met with them in the U.S. and overseas to better understand their businesses and needs. We were still at the ground level.

The next year or so was dedicated to identifying and executing projects to fill their specific needs. Our list continued to grow, and the volume of global revenue grew geometrically.

Over the next several years, revenue from these three initial companies surpassed revenue generated by many of our audit clients. Additional companies and senior partners were added to the experiment, and it began to alter the *audit-centric* culture of the firm to become more *client-centric*.

The larger 30,000 foot vision was accomplished: We grew substantial revenue with well over 100 non-audit clients and added several billion dollars globally.

Piloting at 30,000 feet. Piloting at ground level.

## ourcing Within the U.S.

rly stages of bringing a new product and/or service
don't do everything internally. Consider outsourcing
all but the most essential functions.

Examine the entire spectrum of normal business functions
and evaluate those that are most critical to differentiation and
marketplace success.

There is a surprising array of available consultants and services.
Services can range from upfront marketing and sales to back
office procurement, technology, and legal.

Weigh your most critical, unique elements in the supply chain
and support. Focus on the most important with your internal
hires, and outsource the rest.

Effective outsourcing is a facet of innovation. Focus on the
core that differentiates.

## Anecdote: Outsourcing Within the U.S.

The Gillette Company is renowned for its excellent merchandising and point of purchase displays at its retail locations. In particular, their shaving division "The All Star" promotion was held up as one of the industry's best practices for years. Consumers were asked to vote on their favorite players. Special displays were set up at retail stores. Consequently, it served as the platform for Gillette to introduce innovative new products.

For years, in-store merchandising was the responsibility of the salesforce and became a significant drain of time for a seemingly mundane, lower value-added service. It had to have prior approval at headquarters. So there was little value added at the retail store level.

But then a working mother, who had extensive merchandising experience with Gillette, presented a proposal to take over its in-store merchandising. Gillette accepted, so she recruited and trained a network of other working parents who could conduct in-store merchandising during very flexible hours.

This shaving division merchandising innovation spread to the Paper Mate Division and eventually to other divisions. And what began as a Gillette outsourcing opportunity grew to an in-store merchandising business for the innovative mother and her network of working parents who subsequently served other companies as well.

Consider what is critically important to not only uniquely fill the needs of your customer but to also differentiate from the competition. Weigh the pros and cons.

Consider innovatively outsourcing all but the most essential functions of the business. Focus on differentiation.

# 4. Challenging the Dominant Player

It is ironic that the dominant market leader can often be blind to innovation in its own backyard. Or, that it may be reluctant to cannibalize its own products or services.

There are two opportunities emanating from understanding this phenomenon.

First, upon realizing this, you can set up an independent group within your dominant company to innovate, fulfill needs, and attack your own weaknesses. Become your own disrupter and your own worst enemy. Call it creative self-destruction.

Second, seeing this reluctance in a competitor, you can innovate with a unique product or service. Your competition may be the last to see it coming, and their own blind dominance is your best competitive insulation.

Dominant market leaders: Give yourself a tough look in the mirror.

Innovative disruptors drool. Creative destruction.

## Anecdote: Challenging the Dominant Player

Kodak dominated the consumer photo industry after introducing the Brownie in the early 1900s. It was a fairly simple, accessible camera. Eventually, many other cameras appeared on the market, and they all used photographic film.

Over time, Kodak felt strong competition from its Japanese competitor, Fujifilm. Then came the Polaroid camera with its instantly developed pictures within the camera itself. Kodak became preoccupied with both of these competitive, film-based disruptors.

Next came even higher quality film-based cameras such as those produced by Canon, Leica, Pentax, Minolta, and Sony. Disposable film-based cameras enjoyed popularity for a while, too. An entire industry emerged around cameras using film. Other businesses that produced camera bags and accessories, and photo development shops, greatly benefited from this market.

But who was the real disrupter of this industry? It was an entry that blindsided most everyone: Apple's iPhone and other smartphones.

Instant pictures and results. No film to process and no delays in developing. Portability. Shareability. The device was not only a phone that could take great photos, users could also check email, text friends, peek at the stock market, listen to music, watch videos, and so much more. This level of quality and usability has surpassed our imagination.

Apple does have competitors, and so far, they are able to increase their own market share by disrupting and challenging themselves with improved pixels and quality, modest telephoto capability, movie making, slow motion, and panoramic capability. And a wider viewing screen.

All this was unimaginable a short decade ago, but now we have a mass market. Evolution and disruption.

The disruptor: Apple. And the disruptor challenging itself with its own improvements.

Creative destruction.

# 5. Innovating Through Integration

Innovation can come through many unusual means.

Most companies struggle when it comes to working across their organizational silos due to different organizational functions, divisions, and processes. For some companies, problems are compounded if geography plays a role, and there are divisions in other cities or countries.

If one can master communication and integration across silos, one can find a unique way to serve customers and gain a leg up on the competition.

How can integration be more successful?

INTEGRATING

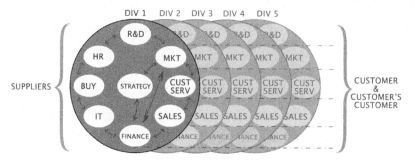

## Anecdote: Innovating Through Integration

As organizations become more complex, innovation through integration becomes increasingly challenging—yet competitively differentiating.

As PricewaterhouseCoopers became increasingly complex with its rapid growth, and as the globe became more tightly interconnected, a service organization that could integrate among its various departments and functions, its divisional lines of service, its processes, and its countries could competitively differentiate itself.

This became a competitive, innovative strategy for PwC in the mid to late 90s. Its focus on key clients became an overriding priority. Positive, innovative behavior dealing with complex client issues was raised up to the highest level of recognition for partners.

Line of service (audit, tax, and consulting for example) became de-emphasized and was replaced by business oriented solutions that, of course, utilized the expertise housed in many lines of service. Internal functions became de-emphasized. Country autonomy was de-emphasized as important clients' needs were raised up to be paramount.

*The mere process of being truly integrated was innovative.* Clients were struggling themselves to achieve this, so they recognized and appreciated it in a major service organization.

# ing Across Divisions

divisions of the same company often call on the
)mer. They often have different sales forces, financial
terms, logistics, customer service departments, and different
locations in other cities or countries.

How can all of these different divisions be better integrated
to help enhance the customer experience?

How can companies provide unique differentiation?

ACROSS DIVISIONS

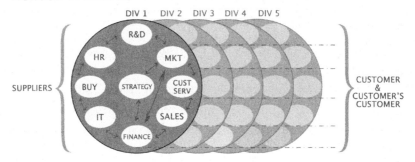

## Anecdote: Working Across Divisions

In the 90s, PepsiCo had a reputation of being quite decentralized by division. Measurement and career success intensified the divisional separation as it was the source for identifying rising star executives.

This meant that the Beverage/Pepsi division operated distinctly differently from Frito Lay/Snacks, and the Restaurant division, which, at the time, consisted of KFC, Taco Bell, and Pizza Hut.

As several new acquisitions (Tropicana and Quaker) added to the complexity of PepsiCo, it became apparent that they needed to alter their singular divisional organization to a strategy and structure that was more *integrated*.

This was accomplished successfully over several years. It allowed more integrated and innovative cooperation among divisions and more coordinated efforts to deal with common customers such as the very large retailers.

The clout that this afforded PepsiCo was immense as they realized they were among the largest product and service providers to many large retailers. At Walmart, for example, PepsiCo's total divisional sales made them the largest provider. It added to the complexity and challenges to integrate across divisions, but PepsiCo knew it afforded aspects of competitive uniqueness and power—especially as Category Management came increasingly into play.

Similarly with Gillette in the UK, they were one of the largest providers to Boots (the dominant drug chain) of total sales of razor blades, toiletries, pens, appliances, dental products, and batteries. Relationship clout ... when effectively combined and integrated.

Competitive innovation and power through *divisional integration*.

# 7. Building an Innovative Network

People innovate ideas. Find like-minded people in an organization and build a network with those who think in a creative and innovative manner. Focus everyone in the network around the customer and being unique.

Start with a few people you know best. Meet, talk, and share "working with customer" success stories.

Plan another meeting, and each of you invite two to three like-minded friends to share customer success stories. Reach out for diverse functional, divisional, and country diversity.

Repeat. The network can build geometrically.

An innovative network can change the culture of an organization.

## Anecdote: Building an Innovative Network

In the mid 1990s, a small group of three interested Price Waterhouse partners, each with Fortune 200 multinational client responsibilities, got together over dinner in London. Their like-minded thinking had them realize the needs of their clients would best be filled if a global, coordinated network could be built to work across borders, lines of service, and the seams of their clients' own silos.

Soon the network grew to over a hundred interested partners and had spread across the U.S., Europe, Asia, and South America. Each partner had become a node, willing to share and innovate around the needs of their clients. If someone ventured into a new country, there was someone to call for a trusted opinion on how to proceed, and who to rely on. There was a similar mindset. Node to node.

While the top management of the firm was aware of this network, it was already effectively working with partners who had direct client responsibility. Client Partners' success hung on the reliability of the network.

These nodes spread across various lines of service (divisions) of the firm, and the network became the envy of other partners who had similar responsibilities. The purpose was to be inclusive if a partner was willing to give as well as take.

The nodes became networks of hundreds of partners and was eventually formally recognized as part of the firm's "Global Ambition" to serve global clients across disciplines and across borders.

As a result, clients recognized Price Waterhouse to be one of the most integrated global service organizations, and this innovative reputation resulted in literally billions in new revenue for the firm.

Node to node. Building an innovative like-minded network.

Change the culture.

# About the Future

out your key customers and what is in store for their
ik about it from the customers' top executive perspective. What do they think and worry about while exercising?
What do they think about while on vacation? What do they want
to talk about?

Go talk to the top executives with your hypotheses. Compare
notes. Listen. Tactfully challenge their thinking. Support your
thoughts on their future with trends you see, read, and think
about.

Both of you will learn and likely shift from your original views.
Out of these conversations will come insights, and insights will
generate innovation. When you talk about the future and pos-
sibilities, you are on more equal footing with your customers'
senior executives.

It's hard to "out know" senior executives on their existing
business. They have all the numbers and internal analysis.

Most executives relish the chance to talk about their future,
especially with someone who has done his or her homework
and is not blinded by internal biases.

Try it. Experiment. Innovation is likely to follow.

Talk about the future.

## Anecdote: Talk About the Future

At PricewaterhouseCoopers, we had completed some successful projects with GE and had begun building good senior executive confidence and relationships as the world was opening up after the Russian Revolution.

Interestingly, several of the senior GE executives in their international group, both finance and operations, had been impressed with our globally connected team. They were open to meet and "just talk about the future." We had done some homework and thinking ourselves and realized that international growth at the time was high on GE's agenda.

We had a candid exchange. We talked about our own PwC expansion and challenges and how we had organized ourselves around a few clients like GE to insure that we would not be siloed by country or internal service lines. They liked our frankness and went on to share some of their future strategies.

As the conversation progressed, they inquired about PwC's strengths in China, India, and Mexico. We knew that we had rapidly expanded in the last several years in China. We had been involved with another client in India and knew the head of our office there, so we could speak comfortably about it. At the time, we were not entirely familiar with our Mexico operations but promised to follow up quickly with an objective assessment.

The future was now. Soon after this meeting, we traveled to China to assess our resources and meet our senior partner. We also reinforced the good relationship with our senior partner in India, and we reached out to Mexico to get to know the senior leadership there.

Within three months, we had projects or GE acquisitions going in all three countries. Within six months, the cover of Fortune magazine had featured GE opening up these and other countries around the world.

Talk about the future. Listen. Challenge. Be candid. Be prepared to shift and act. Innovate.

## nstructing an Industry:
## structing an Enterprise

ndustries are continually going through a process of deconstruction—a process of specialization where the traditional supply chain is being carved out by competition or by specialized components.

Automobile operations were originally vertically integrated from growing rubber for the tires to owning all the dealerships to manufacturing all components of the car in house. Today, the core enterprise is really assembly, design, and marketing operations.

Many industries begin vertically integrated: controlling or owning top to bottom of the supply chain from the front end of the business (sales) to the back end (production and procurement).

Certain components are then broken off (or deconstructed) by competition or intentional outsourcing, leaving the core industry to focus on its uniqueness. These components splinter off to the right with opportunities for someone else to assemble the components into another opportunity.

VERTICAL

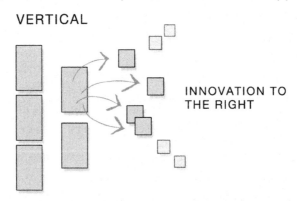

INNOVATION TO
THE RIGHT

Think about the industry you are in or want to attack. Generally, there are innovation opportunities "moving to the right" or increasing specialization of components.

## Anecdote: Deconstructing an Industry: Reconstructing an Enterprise

Apple is a good example of a specialized enterprise even though its focus is on a number of different (but related) products and services. Although it does subcontract and outsource most of its iPhone components to other companies, it tightly maintains its core R&D and marketing.

Apple maintains the innovative aspects of imagining what the customer wants or will value, and it designs the next generation of the product.

But it outsources the chip technology, internal assembly, manufacture of the plastic case, and other components. These outsourcers, some of which are in countries like China, Japan, and Germany, have taken these "farmed out" components and assembled them into a very large business.

Apple has become a specialized enterprise while companies like Foxconn have reconstructed part of an industry.

Ford evolved from originally producing everything for a car (including growing rubber trees for tires, controlling dealerships, and advertising) to distributing through independent dealers, assembling cars with sub-contracted parts, etc.

Deconstruction requires innovation. It takes integration with providers and outsourcers. Look to the right for innovation opportunities and specialization of components.

# 10. Deconstructing Leads to Reconstructing

As an industry deconstructs and is broken down into specialized parts or components, new opportunities can emerge.

This is the reconstruction or reassembly of the splintered components into a collection. Some call this new assembly of components *complements*.

Think about the supply-chain used in manufactured clothing.

Originally, U.S. manufacturers made everything in-house. Then hundreds of Chinese subcontracting textile shops sprung up. One company, Lehn & Fink, emerged and cast an organization net over these disparate companies in order to more effectively manage them.

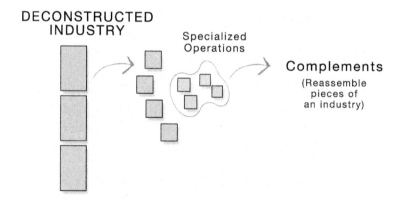

DECONSTRUCTED
INDUSTRY

Specialized
Operations

Complements

(Reassemble
pieces of
an industry)

Innovation can bring fractionalized or "splintered" elements together. The Internet can help.

This is reconstruction, or the creation of new complements.

Etsy is a prime example in an innovative, reconstructed industry.

Long considered a cottage industry, the craft business is splintered across the world. Products are typically produced in people's homes and then taken to local and regional craft shows where the artists display and sell their work—often on tables under tents.

In 2005, Etsy reconstructed this splintered industry by harnessing the power of the Internet. It introduced its e-commerce website to provide a virtual location as well as resources for artists to display and sell their work, regardless of physical location.

Etsy offers a reliable payment system, shipping, user comments, and has also served as a network where artists can discover one another and work together. For example, a painter or photographer who wants to focus on just producing the canvas or the photo can link up with someone who specializes in matting and framing to provide a completed work ready for display.

Etsy has gained popularity internationally, too. An artist who once only attended local craft fairs now has the ability to sell work across borders.

Reconstruction is as innovative as the process of deconstruction. It requires one to be observant and look for trends in a particular industry so that opportunities can be anticipated and acted upon.

Reassembly of the un-assembled components, or complements.

Another fresh view of innovation.

# nding Beyond Experiences

: we can go to one restaurant and pay $30 for a filet d to another and pay $60 for the same cut? And after the latter restaurant, declare it was a good deal and a great experience?

It is beyond the product or service itself. It's the atmosphere. The view. The service with an engaging and attentive waiter. Fine china, glassware, and white tablecloth. The presentation of the food itself.

It's often the *staging* of a total experience.

There is a new economy that has emerged around us documented in a famous book titled *The Experienced Economy* by Pine and Gilmore.

One major significance is that people will pay more for a meaningful experience. Higher pricing.

## Anecdote: Extending Beyond Experiences

Assuming there is perceived value, people are willing to pay for experiences.

The Walt Disney Company has expanded the concept of amusement park rides and attractions to include accommodations, fun for parents as well as children, clean facilities, attractive and smiling people—all of which adds up to a total experience—and an upcharge of 300 to 400%. "But worth it!"

Not long ago, an average child's birthday party cost the price of a box of Betty Crocker cake mix and an egg—say around $2.50.

Today, parents are purchasing "Build-a-Bear" and "American Girl" parties that can easily run $600 or more, packaged with lunch or tea, including instructions on how to write a thank you note. It's all part of the experience—and many are willing to pay for it.

Travelers themselves can arrange a trip to Africa over the Internet for under $10,000 by booking flights, renting equipment, and securing lodging by themselves.

Or people can use a travel agent to arrange first class accommodations and food, professional safaris that assure prime animal viewing and photography opportunities, and private flights to assure efficient transportation between camps. $25,000 to $40,000 per couple may seem steep, yet for a once in a lifetime experience, it can be worth the difference in price. Safety. Meeting locals. Customer service. All part of the price.

Appropriately staged and authentically presented experiences typically justify an up-charge and provide pricing flexibility to the provider.

Innovating experiences is one of the  innovations of the last decade or two—and our imagination to conceive is likely to be the only limit. Meaningful experiences.

Higher pricing likely.

# ing—Items for Rent

1other area where innovation is all around us, but we
s see it. Where might it take us?

Our car sits idle much of the day. What about a rental by day?
(Hertz and Avis.) What about by the hour? (Zipcar.) Just when I
need it and maybe even unlicensed like a traditional taxi? (Uber.)

Or a vacation home? (I can only get two weeks away.) Or my
office? I travel 50% of the time, so it sits empty. (Office hotel-
ing.) My secretary? (Only need the person effectively 30% of the
time.) My nanny? (Can I effectively share her or him with another
family?)

The concept of sharing has great innovative applications, especially as we are pressed for time and pressed economically.

Find some time to think about this creatively.

Sharing.

## Anecdote: Sharing—Items for Rent

Sharing high-priced goods has been greatly enhanced by the Internet thanks to its broad global audience. Times are changing.

Only a few short years ago, designer clothing, as well as clothing used for limited or special occasions like weddings or proms, was either ultra expensive or difficult to find.

Rent the Runway found a way to address this need online. Customers can browse thousands and thousands of photos for the perfect dress, chat with a stylist if needed, order, and then receive the desired dress at one's doorstep within a few days. After wearing the dress, it is mailed back, cleaned, and readied for the next customer. In effect, it has been rented or shared for a fraction of the cost. Truly innovative.

Traveling can be expensive, but Airbnb has taken the hassle out of finding a place to stay through its community that focuses on sharing spaces or accommodations.

Registering online with Airbnb allows members to list and book unique accommodations across the globe. For the provider, it lessens the hassle of marketing or advertising, hashing out reservations details, making confirmations, and collecting payments. For the person seeking reservations, it easy to search for and book destination accommodations.

Think about fixed assets and durable goods. There may be many innovative ways to share and spread the costs using rentals. Aspects of this practice have been around for years, but the Internet and portability of the smartphone are bringing new dimensions and creativity.

Sharing.

Economical. Portable. Innovative.

# 13. Focus on Heavy Users

A successful innovator comes to know the best users. The loyal users. The frequent users. The earlier triers and/or adapters. The repeaters. The heavy users.

Each of these categories is important. Each has different characteristics to observe and track.

Appreciate that the early adopters may not always be repeaters. And not all repeaters will become heavy users.

Come to know your heavy users. Keep them happy. Really listen to them. Coddle them. They are your gold!

Frequently, they are a minority—even a small minority. And market research will often miss them.

Heavy users. Repeat: *They are gold.*

## Anecdote: Focus on Heavy Users

Here are a few quick examples of how paying attention to the heavy users can benefit a market.

Razor blades: A minority of users really loved Wilkinson's Bonded Razor and used the blades quite frequently. They became repeat, heavy users.

Other toiletry products: A woman with long hair may use three to five times the shampoo of a man with short hair, so consider usage.

Food products: Certain foods, like popcorn and snacks, might be consumed five or ten times more by a heavy user than that of a light user. Beer or soft drink consumption is also characterized by heavy user market segments. Put them together and we see very high consumption.

Experience visitations: Parents with children in a certain age group are more likely to visit Disney more often. Restaurants with a particular cuisine are likely to have heavy users versus the casual, less frequent customer. Singles or retired couples are more likely to be heavy travelers and repeaters for certain kinds of trips or experiences.

Sometimes a heavy user can be worth five, ten, or fifteen times more than an occasional or casual customer—get to know them, pay attention to their feedback, and market to their needs.

Analyze the heavy user. This is an important and often missed aspect of innovation.

# 14. Capitalizing on Satisfaction Gaps

In most product and service categories, there are subtle (and some not-so-subtle) gaps between what customers really want and what they will accept.

I prefer a close shave but don't want to bleed all over the sink.

I want to stop at McDonalds but will accept Burger King.

I desire a rare steak but will settle for medium.

I like a smooth wine but will accept a slightly acidic wine.

I prefer morning golf tee time but will take afternoon.

I want objective financial planning but it's tied to product sales.

And in the services industry, "not easy to work with" is one of the most frequently cited shortcomings when customers talk about providers. Often very subtle and hard to read.

Identification of these gaps is not easily market researched. Often the customer has put up with a compromise for too long.

Think about this in a category you are familiar with. Observe. What are people putting up with? What are the subtle or not-so-subtle compromises?

This is the "Satisfaction Gap."

Find an innovative way to fill the need.

## *Anecdote: Capitalizing on Satisfaction Gaps*

One of the first free and publicly available video conferencing tools was Skype. There were other providers for the corporate market, but most users experienced significant transmission hesitation and delays. The visual image could be jerky and inconsistent, and sometimes the audio would cut out.

The original video conferencing phenomenon was so unusual and innovative that many users were willing to live with this "satisfaction gap" and found the compromises acceptable—at least initially.

In 2006, Cisco's TelePresence solved a number of video conferencing issues, although initially the cost was quite high and many organizations could only justify a few of the TelePresence sites.

Watching and listening to others on a large screen, high-definition TV was almost like having the person in the room, and with multiple screens, a conference assembling individuals from around the country or internationally was pretty remarkable and innovative.

Apple's FaceTime further closed the satisfaction gap for the average user with its latest technology available on computers, iPads, and iPhones. The original jerky qualities have all but been eliminated, and the sound quality and picture are close to real time.

Identifying the satisfaction gaps in categories and businesses you are familiar with can be an exciting exercise.

Make notes. Keep a list. This is a strategy and observation opportunity to build new and unique business opportunities.

# 15. Optimizing Intelligent Data

Today, versus five, 10, or even 15 years ago, there is *intelligent data* or "Big Data" to help a provider (product manufacturer or service provider) target its customers.

One can trace the demographic, buying patterns, or even psychological (psychographic) profile of their best customers.

Or trace and influence their buying patterns right at decision time or point of purchase.

Think of the advantage you have if you know your customer well and in person. Think of selling something to a good friend. You know their previous buying habits, patterns, related personal interests, and characteristics or needs that might at first seem unrelated.

If you can imagine this . . . think intelligent data.

## Anecdote: Optimizing Intelligent Data

One of the earliest innovators for intelligent data you order a book on the Civil War, for example, you book recommendations on other war or history to War I or Lincoln. You will also see a "Customers Who Bought This Item Also Bought..." section. Amazon offers many ways to customize search results to best serve the customer.

A similar concept applies to music. If you order or choose the Boston Pops station, you will receive recommendations or "next song selection" for light classical or popular opera. If you order bluegrass or country, you might be prompted to try John Denver's *Country Roads* or a Garth Brooks hit.

Intelligent data is both a service to the end user, or consumer, and a business builder for the provider. Intelligent data can capture and observe trends and habits that even the user may be unaware of. It's also being applied to the food industry, retail shopping, clothing styles, sunglass selection, and many other industries.

Credit card fraud is often detected using similar techniques. A user's buying patterns and geographic locations are observed. Multiple city purchases at more than two locations many hundreds of miles apart on the same day may trigger suspicion. Stores that are not commonly frequented by the user can trigger suspicion as well. Exceptionally large dollar amount purchases can also cause a red flag.

With intelligent data, it is possible to tailor your product or service to the needs of the customer. One key to profitability is to tailor the product as little as necessary—yet to as large a segment as possible.

If this is easy to imagine, think intelligent data.

Think customization.

# 6. Be There . . . Without Really Being There

Given new technology, it is now possible to be there "without being there."

Distributed knowledge from the Internet and high resolution screens are transforming aspects of our physical presence.

Global and other sprawling organizations can have quality meetings and an in-person feel without actually being there. This is especially true for internal meetings. And now, even client meetings with established relationships are being used effectively.

From retirement home visits by distant children to grandparent visits with FaceTime technology to international meetings and conferences—we can be there without being there.

This is a new frontier. What is the right mix of truly being present versus now being "streamed in?" How does one truly connect? What are the ramifications of the historical importance of personal relationships?

Where will the reality of "being there without really being there" take us?

Innovation with today's technology is limitless.

## Anecdote: Be There . . . Without Really Being There

Less than a decade ago, it seemed like science fiction to imagine consumers talking with family members using the technology now broadly available with iPhone's FaceTime.

While Skype was available, it was quite jerky and transmission left a lot to be desired. Now an entire generation of children are growing up accepting distant audiovisual family visits by phone as commonplace.

Companies like Dependa have taken this technology and applied it, so elderly parents can be in touch with out-of-town children, daily. It uses a high resolution TV screen, which many elderly are familiar with and brings a quality image for conversation or even game playing and staying in touch. Medical prescriptions and other basic health care can be administered as well.

Corporations have taken the same capabilities to an even higher level. Cisco's Telepresence has the capability of transmitting high resolution teleconferences with people sitting around the conference table and include close up visuals as they are talking. Charts can be hand drawn and clearly shown, and more formal presentations are easily transmitted, too.

While we might think of this as generally available for only internal meetings, I was recently introduced to the Senior Partner of one of the largest law firms via a Telepresence conference. We became so engaged in this introductory meeting that a 20 minute call went for over an hour. Both of us saved a day's travel!

Being there (without really being there) is a new reality. Innovation is just starting to be applied. The sky's the limit.

# 17. Imagining

Take the simple word "imagine."

Listen for situations where it is appropriate to "imagine if...."

It takes the discussion to a future state. It doesn't attempt to solve the problem or answer the challenge, but it does get others to think about it as well.

Observe how the team works together to find a solution. A future state. A positive effort to achieve the desired end goal.

Imagining: a powerful way to reframe the conversation and focus.

## Anecdote: Imagining

The relatively simple concept of asking people to *imagine* something can have surprising results.

PwC had a tradition of taking its partners to first class venues where partners and their spouses could relax, get to know one another, better understand the business, and mix work with fun.

The tradition had a serious one-day business meeting where the partners would meet in small groups of 15-20 and discuss the nature of the partnership's business and challenges. At the start of this meeting, everyone would go around the table and introduce themselves, typically like this: "I am from____ (city) and work in the____ (audit tax, consulting , etc) part of the practice.

In one meeting, we asked ourselves to *imagine* introducing ourselves by the client(s) we served. There was a long silence. We prided ourselves on a "client centered culture," but this was not how we introduced ourselves. In fact, where we lived and what part of the firm we practiced in was all about us—not about the client.

The conversation this sparked was quite remarkable. It took us to a future state of where we wanted to be. Not only in the U.S. but also globally as many of our clients didn't care if we were in Boston, St. Louis, or San Francisco—they wanted us "out there" where the issues were. And they wanted business people solving problems, not someone who was only representing a siloed part of the practice.

Imagining a future state helped lead the firm to evolve to a more integrated client business orientation. It took us global. It took us out of our internal organization and into the mindset of our customers and clients.

Try imagining. It may take you to some interesting places.

# 18. Implementing and Executing

One big part of innovation is coming up with new ideas, concepts, and prospective products and/or services.

But an equally important (and sometimes undervalued) aspect is implementation and execution to the marketplace.

Action is important: a rigorous plan to commercialization and proactive project management. Contingency plans. Competitive awareness and anticipated reactions.

Experimentation. Testing. Review. Changes. More experimentation. Then implementation.

Commercialization brings together all the business elements from marketing to sales, operations, procurements, logistics, and finance.

Most of us can't do this by ourselves. What skills do we need in-house? Can we afford in-house costs before revenue comes in? What can we cleverly outsource initially?

Generating ideas and concepts is important.

Implementing is next up!

## Anecdote: Implementing and Executing

Most consumer products go through a rigorous phase of discovery and marketplace development, plus there is the time it takes to develop the actual product during R&D. This is only a small part of implementation.

There is often considerable time testing the product itself with consumers to be sure it performs, but there is also time spent advertising and campaign testing to validate a product's "pull." And now, given the importance of social media and the difficulty of containing it to geographic test markets, this has become even more challenging.

There is also an effort through the sales department to insure the retail trade will take on the product, properly merchandise it, and price it properly.

The manufacturing department has to be sure the product can be manufactured in scale, not only for test market but assuming a national launch. Scalability is important. Logistics have to be considered as well—the product must travel well and arrive safely.

Further work is often needed to gauge repeat purchase and consumption usage, and assess potential heavy users.

Perhaps most importantly, there is finance—everything must work together to make a profit.

So implementation (and the details surrounding it) are important to innovation, although not as sexy (and often underestimated).

# Innovative Observations

# 19. Observing as an Art

Most successful innovators have a keen sense of observation.

The good news is that it's an art, and it can be improved at almost any level.

Take time out. Put yourself in listen and receive mode.

Look around you. Make time to do this when you are alone. Observe what is innovative. Make notes.

Keep a list of innovations you've observed.

Set the goal of at least one "observation exercise" per day.

Review your list each week. Have the quality of your observations improved over time?

Ask a like-minded friend or business colleague to try this exercise and compare notes. You'll have fun and get better at observing.

Innovation is all around us. Look for it.

All of us can do this. And it improves with practice.

## Anecdote: Observing as an Art

Late in my career, I began testing a hypothesis about how I observed innovation and found that I had been doing it all along. I just didn't write down my observations.

When you have the opportunity, observe "line management" while standing in an "I" formation in front of an ATM machine at a bank. Not too many years ago, we would line up in three separate lines in front of each one only to be frustrated by choosing the wrong line and watch the next one over move faster. In Russia, by contrast, I observed that they have little respect for lines. Waiting for service in a grocery store or in a passport line, people would butt in and move to the front. Quietly observe the innovation around us. What do we really see and take in?

Once I made a point to write my observations down, I found that they came even easier. In fact, my observations got better. They got deeper, more imaginative. It was so revealing that I tried it on my first group of MBA students.

Remarkably, within two to three weeks, nearly all of the students' abilities to make and record their observations improved. I could see their growing self-confidence in stretching themselves—especially when I had them bring their observations to class to share with everyone. By the end of each school term, virtually 100% "got it." Year after year.

Even more impressive was when certain students began making the connections from these observations to their own powers of innovation. We would use these "transfers" of observations in class to outright innovations. The students would learn from one another—not just from me.

This informal experiment reaffirmed my belief that observing innovation is in fact teachable and learnable. The sample size of nearly 500 students from as many as 30 different countries is fairly reliable, especially with the high percentage of accomplishment.

Observe innovation around you. Look for it. Record it.

41

## 20. Realizing Most Entrepreneurs Are Innovative, but Not All Innovators Are Entrepreneurs

This is fairly straightforward if you think about it. Entrepreneurs are starting a business or bringing something new to the marketplace.

Many innovative, creative people work for others. They are in a small or large businesses. The real question is, how can you generate, refine, and bring new products or services to the market?

One important point here is that, early on in your career (or if you are somewhat inexperienced), you can learn on someone else's nickel.

Learn the basics of business.

Experiment with your ideas and contribute.

This is a win-win.

Call me an innovator? Call me an entrepreneur?

## Anecdote: Realizing Most Entrepreneurs Are Innovative, But Not All Innovators Are Entrepreneurs

While leading innovation teams at Wilkinson, Noxell, Gillette, and PwC, I realized that we could inspire team members from different functional areas in a company to become more innovative. These areas included marketing, sales, operations, finance, R&D, human resources, and information technology.

We would invite people from different functional areas to be a part of our team and then talk with our customers first hand. Each team member would pick up on the needs of the client from a different perspective (depending on whether his or her specialty was sales, finance, operations, or IT, for example) and then lend his or her individual skills to construct solutions.

After 12 years working for large companies, I dove into becoming an entrepreneur with two partners who greatly *complemented* my strengths. We co-founded the Consumer Financial Institute (CFI), which eventually became the largest independent provider of financial planning in the United States. Instead of catering to the wealthy, CFI targeted the middle income family.

Although our company started small, we realized that most of the skills needed to be innovative were, in fact, common to both those in larger companies as well as those in smaller start-ups.

Regardless of size, though, like-minded innovators can find ways to bridge the disparities often found between small and large companies.

Innovation can take place in any size organization.

It's not the size as much as the *attitude*.

# 21. Handling a Customer ... or a Client?

Is there a difference?

Yes. If we think of a *client* as one associated with an ongoing relationship and repeat purchase a client is more likely to be an annuity.

A *customer* is typically someone who tries or buys a product or service. Repeat is not assured, and the product or service must fulfill expectations.

Professional service firms typically think of clients in terms of an ongoing or continuing relationship.

Think of what it will take for the first time "trier" to become a client and have an ongoing relationship whether it is based on a product, service, or experience.

Can a single word make a difference and lead to a cultural shift and more innovation? Some companies are finding the answer: *YES*.

## Anecdote: Handling a Customer ... or a

There can be a difference in the way a word is perc the distinction between *customer* and *client* can have how we conduct business.

Customers are typically thought of as short-term. They buy something and leave. They may return another day to buy something else, but there isn't typically a meaningful or sustained relationship between the vendor and the customer.

Gillette, Pepsico, Procter & Gamble, as well as IBM, historically used the term customer when referring to someone who bought their products and services. There was often a connotation of opposition or competition—a "win-lose" relationship between the vendor and the customer: "Sell them something, even if it is more than what they need."

A customer might be a retailer or large company.

Price Waterhouse referred to the people who bought its products and services as *clients*. Clients have long-term relationships, and the dynamics of the relationship feel more vested, more personal. A certain amount of trust develops.

IBM purchased the PwC consulting business in 2002, and a few years later, the president of IBM began referring to its customers as clients in all internal communications, as well as in its Annual Report. The culture began to shift as this difference became clearer, and *certain behaviors were reinforced.*

After changing its terminology and incorporating some PwC practices, IBM noticed that its clients came to increasingly trust their proposals and solutions. For those partners skilled in this approach the truly authentic, loyal clients could sense a difference and would acknowledge an improved working relationship. Over time, this resulted in an improved fee relationship.

Pick your innovative words carefully. Client or customer?

## 2. Adjusting Attitude

None of us wake up feeling great every day. But think about those around us who sincerely appear to feel good every day.

It's remarkable how people are drawn to (and want to be around) a positive attitude. It creates an atmosphere of "Can Do" and "Let's Try It!" It creates, essentially, an innovative environment.

You can choose your attitude. Decide how you want to be and you will be.

You can act your way into it on a bad day. Practice it. It will become authentic.

Try an attitude adjuster.

Innovation follows the right, positive attitude.

## Anecdote: Adjusting Attitude

I arrived each day at CFI feeling that we were on the forefront of revolutionizing the financial planning industry. As companies such as IBM, Chevron, and P&G came aboard to customize our service for their special needs, the positive atmosphere was real and contagious for all internal employees. It was exciting to be on the cutting edge, and it helped create a positive attitude.

Being self-starting is another way to adjust attitude. CFI was underway, and we wanted to share our success story in the national media. We were soon on national television and print media with complimentary coverage of our story.

This increased our confidence, which spread throughout the organization as an attitude adjuster. Confidence is contagious.

At PwC, team members on the GE, PepsiCo, and Gillette accounts were inspired by our positive and contagious attitude. There were the inevitable disappointments, but the CAN DO attitude of team members created an *esprit de corps* that would solve any problems or issues that came along.

Think about the work environment you thrive in. Think about the positive environments you can create.

"Your *attitude* determines your *altitude*," says John Sullivan, a close colleague of mine. The right altitude provides innovative perspective.

# 23. Transferring Innovations

It's one thing to have the skill to observe innovation around us.

It's another thing to have the skill to transfer it from one category, industry, or situation to another.

It's using analogies. It's using the expression, "if this, then that."

Practice it. Look for innovation and success in one category and observe how it's been transferred to another.

Then, take your list of original observations and imagine how it can be transferred to another category. Practice this art.

Rise up to 30,000 feet (big picture thinking) with an observation and conceptualize it. At a high level, it's often easier to see a transferable quality.

Surprisingly few innovations are completely original. Often, there is some transfer across from another innovation.

Practice makes perfect.

## Anecdote: Transferring Innovations

It is fairly easy to find examples where an innovation in one place inspired innovation in another. The hospitality industry is famous for continually innovating and reinventing itself.

Finer hotels will typically stage an experience for its "guests." At a Ritz-Carlton, for example, each lobby is designed to create an impression, and staff are purposefully trained to provide a specific experience for its high-end customers. For example, if a guest asks where the pool is, he or she is accompanied, not just directed, to the pool, or *point of resolution*. The employee "owns" the issue.

At other hotels, there may be a theme running through the entire property reflecting the highlights of its location or culture. At a Disney hotel, for instance, the theme might be "family fun and friendly." Again, staff are trained to be a part of the stage and help create a particular experience for their guests.

Similarly, when you walk through the door at the McLean Hardware in McLean, Virginia, a representative will greet you, make sure any questions you have are being addressed, and accompany you to the section of the store where the product you are looking for is located.

The hardware employee will engage you in dialogue to be sure he or she understands your need or project and might even offer a few handy tips. If it is very specialized, the employee may ask a colleague to join in the conversation to be sure you get the best advice possible.

Transferring innovations. Hotel to hardware. It works. Look for it.

Practice it.

## 24. Presenting as an Art

Innovators are always presenting. Convincing people. It is a form of selling.

Innovators need to convince everyone around them. Whether it is their customers, investors, employees, or suppliers, they are always on.

Some of the most effective presentations are not business presentations in the traditional sense but dialogue—questions and answers, discussion and eye contact.

Use props and visuals if needed. And yes, there can be bullets and pictures on the screen, or in a brief "deck" for organization and outline along with key take-away points.

But ultimately, your best presentation is discussion. Dialogue. Engage with your audience. Find something to make them smile or laugh. Make a real connection.

Actually, if you find something that you personally find sincerely amusing or laughable and share it, you will smile or even laugh.

It will relax your audience. Then they are yours.

## Anecdote: Presenting as an Art

After appearing on the Today Show to talk about financial planning with CFI, NBC called me back to see if I would be interested in doing a segment on how people could prepare themselves for *retirement.*

Though very excited to participate, I do remember struggling to find an analogy or prop that could help make the segment come alive and be memorable.

At four in the morning, I woke up in the hotel with an idea. I walked down the hall in search of a janitor's closet. Sure enough, I found exactly what I needed: a bucket. An *orange* bucket.

The next morning on *The Today Show*, Jane Pauley introduced me, and after talking for a minute or so, I pulled out the big orange bucket. Jane, who didn't know I had a prop, looked horrified. She glanced over at her producer to see how to handle it, but I launched right into my analogy.

"Preparing for retirement finances is like trying to fill a leaky bucket," I said. "You want to go into retirement with a sufficient and rising level of water (money), but a lot of it will leak out in retirement."

Jane started listening and was engaged. She asked compelling questions and it turned out to be quite a meaningful segment.

For years after that segment, in conversations around retirement, people would comment, "*Oh*, so you were the guy with the leaky, orange bucket!"

There is great (and lasting) value in using a good prop during a presentation.

Props. Dialogue. Engagement.

Presenting is an art.

# 25. Making Someone Happy

If we think about making someone happy, it gets us outside of ourselves. We can better listen—and observe—who we are interacting with.

If we sense where *they* are (and where *they* are coming from), we can essentially discover their needs. This can lead to innovation.

Think about this process and practice it with friends, family, and customers.

It's important to take action. Once you sense a need, do something about it—however small.

Go out of your way. It will put a smile on their face. It's a part of team building and creating a caring, innovative atmosphere for colleagues and customers.

Make someone happy. It can lead to innovation.

## Anecdote: Making Someone Happy

It's often the small things we do each day for one another that become part of our personna. Maybe these acts of kindness or caring don't seem like a big deal, but they are critical to our relationships—a step toward being innovative. It gets us outside ourselves.

Jim and Lee are two friends from my college days at Brown. Lee became a successful real estate lawyer in Virginia and the greater D.C. Metro area. He has given me loads of advice and insight related to my real estate interests over the years but has never sent me a bill. Jim became a noted pediatrician in Hingham, Massachusetts and would never take a payment for the care he provided my family in neighboring Scituate.

Jim and Lee both love golf—a passion all three of us still share. Streamsong, a new golf course billed as the "Pebble Beach of Florida," recently opened up. We agreed to meet and play the course for several days. Even though they could both easily afford it, I picked up the tab. When they found out, they were so appreciative, it made their day—and was just one small, symbolic way I could repay their kindness.

Matt, a senior executive at Pepsico, and I had done a lot of business together over the years. One day we discovered we had gone to rival schools. He went to Georgetown Prep, while I attended Landon in the Maryland suburbs. We made a friendly bet on the outcome of an upcoming football game, and Georgetown won. I decided to get a Prep blanket with Georgetown school logo on it and present it to him. It almost brought tears to his eyes for no other reason than I had been thoughtful enough to make time to get the blanket and acknowledge his team and alma mater.

Make an effort to make someone's day. It is not difficult if you think about what that person likes or what might be special to him or her.

It gets you outside yourself—and this is important to innovation.

# 26. Respecting the Absurd Idea

If we hear an absurd idea, we often have one of two reactions:

1: It's a stupid idea, we dismiss it, and go onto another idea or topic

*or*

2: It's so far out there that it frees up other thinking and ideation. It is now less risky to bring out other unusual ideas.

The absurd idea needs to be treasured and coddled. It needs to be protected and respected.

Creating an acceptable environment for the absurd idea often frees people up and allows them to take risks. They can have greater confidence in their own thinking and ideas.

Encourage and protect the absurd idea.

It may not be all that absurd but instead contain the seed of a well intended, valuable idea. Honor it.

Write it down. Save it. Then continue.

## Anecdote: Respecting the Absurd Idea

An "essential paradox" often comes into play when we explore ideas. How can seemingly opposed things live together? How can opposites be in harmony?

At Wilkinson, we debated over initial findings that consumers could not rationalize how they were able to get "a closer shave" without nicking themselves. As simple as it sounds, *more close* yet *comfortable* was a paradox because consumers had yet to experience it.

More often than not, true innovation uproots traditional mindsets—and that can cause revolutions in categories. This is part of the paradox.

Can we easily imagine a camera without film? Can we imagine having the instantaneous ability to capture an image or an event and then erase it if we don't like it? Years ago, this might have seemed like an absurd idea—something we may have read about in a science fiction novel, perhaps.

Yet today, many people carry a smartphone device that can snap photos, record videos and voice memos, remind us of important appointments, play our favorite songs, check email, text friends, connect through Facetime with our children and grandchildren, find good restaurants, pay bills, read books and magazines, check the weather, navigate, and much, much more.

Absurd ideas can lead to great things. Absurd ideas are worth exploring. Don't be too quick to judge or dismiss what might seem like a crazy idea.

Write it down before you cast it aside. Seeds of innovation.

# 27. Pricing Innovatively

Innovative pricing is not new. But technology and new services enabled by recent developments and innovative thinking are opening up new avenues.

There are five new wave pricing opportunities:

- freemium and subscription based,
- peak usage—using RFID chip technology,
- experience based,
- bundling, and
- concierge or retainer.

Several of these developments may not at first seem revolutionary since we have become initially familiar with them through other means. For example, magazines have historically been subscription based versus an individual newsstand price.

Airline seat pricing based on peak demands have been around. This phenomenon was initially facilitated by big data computer capabilities allowing peak loading and instantaneous profit calculations around supply and demand.

But now there are some important new twists.

We see innovative pricing opportunities and transfers from successes in unlikely places and circumstances.

Let's look at some specific examples.

## Anecdote: Pricing Innovatively

Some of the more interesting developments that br[ ] techniques into focus are Internet services like Netfl[ ] Amazon.

Netflix streams movies on demand via electronic ordering. Rather than paying for individual movies, one can pay a flat subscription rate and view an unlimited number of movies in a certain time frame (usually per month).

There is similar monthly pricing for Spotify and Sirius for music. Innovators created "freemium" pricing: where monthly subscriptions are free, but the service includes advertising. For a premium price, one can get the same music without the annoyance and interruption of ads.

Amazon now bundles free shipping in their premium service, Amazon Prime. It locks customers in.

Peak usage pricing has been enabled in innovative ways thanks to radio-frequency identification (RFID) chips. For example, limited toll roads in Washington, D.C. and other metro areas now charge premium toll access during peak travel commuter times. The same section of road might cost $5.00 at peak traffic times but only $1.00 when less busy. The advantage goes to the busy traveler.

Another example of peak pricing and chip technology can be seen in Colorado. In the Vail ski area, customers can bundle faster ticket scanning (fewer lines) with tracking one's vertical feet skied, mountain photo opportunities, and food discounts by using the PEAKS rewards program with a "pass card."

Doctors are using concierge pricing to insure access. Retainers, historically used by lawyers, help insure access as well and also promote loyalty. Ultimately, concierge pricing and retainers may increase profitability in this rapidly changing environment.

Look for other pricing innovation examples in restaurants, entertainment, and other experiences that are purposely staged to create higher perceived value.

# 28. Serving Few to Many

Think of the many things that have been available only to a few:

- higher education and the best professors;
- medical care and the best doctors;
- business insights from the best CEOs;
- tricky legal issues and the best lawyers;
- important trends observed by the best management; consultants, and thought leaders; and
- best audio and visual performances and best performers.

What is available today to only a relative few?

Is this a fertile area for innovation?

What can be expanded?

What are the business implications?

Who will resist the change?

Who might best come in and disrupt?

Can it be made available to all?

## Anecdote: Serving Few to Many

The education industry is experiencing innovative transformation through Massive Open Online Courses (MOOCs). Organizations like Coursera, Kahn Academy, Ed-X, and TED are bringing the knowledge of experts to a large—oftentimes worldwide—audience.

MIT's freshman class can take an online Ed-X Biology course presented by one of its leading professors. Over 10,000 participants have taken this course, and not all of them were MIT freshman—attendance came from many countries around the world.

MOOCs are forcing educators to consider tuition and the trade-off of offering free courses. There are also educators who believe MOOCs should be combined with in-person classroom time to have maximum impact and reliable testing results.

This is fine tuning. The concept is out and being further tested.

Famous professors at many leading universities like Stanford, University of Virginia, Harvard, and MIT are sharing their courses.

Information that was historically available to only a few is now available to all. Watch for experiments combining in-person with remote.

One of the more innovative ways of distributing knowledge is through the organization providing TED Talks.

TED brings the most forward thinking individuals to discuss many thousands of topics to a widely distributed audience. Topics range from the latest educational best practices in India to Microsoft's Bill Gates delivering 20 minutes on professional career measurement and from the future of brain research and how we think to the effect of new video technology on the future of cultural centers' live performance halls.

Innovation: making information available to all.

# 29. Reaching Globally

Today, an innovation can have almost instant global reach.

And fortunately, for now, English is still the universal business language.

So when you think about the broad spectrum of a potential market, it is valuable to consider the entire globe—especially given the Internet's reach. Practical considerations related to currency, pricing, shipping, legal issues, cultural differences, and more add complications but can be properly addressed to reach full potential and scale.

Can you think of half a dozen industries that have recently become global, or are increasingly likely to become global in the near future?

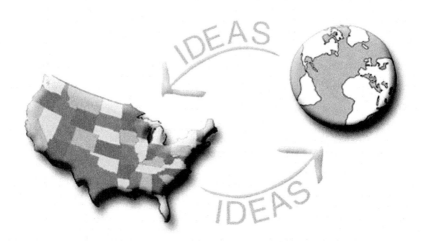

## Anecdote: Reaching Globally

One example of the power of global reach takes place in the gaming industry. Many online games, like Zynga's FarmVille, are free to play and players can earn *virtual money* by building and maintaining a virtual farm. In order to reach higher levels in the game, players can spend the "Farm Cash" they earn, and can purchase more "Farm Cash" by spending real money.

Part of what made this game so popular across the globe is its connection to Facebook. When FarmVille appeared in 2009, players shared their progress and could solicit help from other Facebook friends. It was the most popular game on Facebook for about two years.

Card games, Scrabble, poker—virtually any gambling game is expandable to the Internet globally. Add in the ability to use a service like PayPal or another means of establishing credit, and players can exchange funds. The sky's the limit.

Etsy, a popular website designed to help artists sell their crafts on the Internet, has buyers and sellers in many countries and has had to learn to adapt to the needs needs of its global reach.

Virtually every category is affected by this global reach—including more conservative industries such as education, accounting, law, and medicine.

Innovative ideas flow both ways: into and out of the U.S.

# 30. Innovating via Iterations

Thinking of innovation as a series of iterations allows a certain rhythm and reflection.

We might think of the idea generation and refinement process as a series of iterations. Generate. Record. Reflect. Revisit. Build on the ideas.

This is one aspect of iterations and the creative process.

Another dimension of effective iterations is getting to market and experimentation. This is an important part of what is also now being called "design thinking."

Real life feedback offers a chance to learn and make adjustments. Adjust the product or service offering, the marketing or sales program, the operational aspects, and so forth.

Thinking of successful innovation as a series of steps recognizes the difficult task of getting everything right.

There is a rhythm. Expect obstacles and learning.

Meaningful innovation seldom happens the first time through.

## Anecdote: Innovating via Iterations

Our Personal Financial Report at CFI underwent three to four changes a year during our first few years. Artificial intelligence was at the forefront of the technology we were using, and it kept improving with each iteration.

We could run thousands of personalized reports that accounted for couples with children, different ages of parents and children, different tax situations or investment scenarios, inflation assumptions, etc. Scenarios kept getting more detailed and more accurate as time went on, and we invested more time and expertise into the technology.

Also, think about how smartphones and tablets quickly appeared and evolved over the past few years. The first iPhone was released in June of 2007, and the first iPad was available to the public on April 4, 2010.

But since then, both have gone through a series of iterations that improve the functionality of the devices and improve the user experience. In a highly competitive (and lucrative) market, changes are necessary.

SAP, a German company started by several former IBM employees back in 1972, and other software producers know that process work is rarely fully perfected—especially at launch. Over time, they can get closer to perfection and can tailor software to each client's situation. Almost all of these systems experience a series of releases with improvements and even bug fixes.

Nearly every category rewards early entry to a marketplace with acceptable quality. The iterations of innovation and improvement come later.

# 31. Advertising vs. PR: The Innovator's Choice

One surprisingly easy way to get free, positive public relations (PR) is to have a unique story to tell.

If you have fulfilled a need uniquely, you have a fresh story. You are an innovator.

Most news writers and television producers start each day with a blank page. They are looking for news, some unique angle—something fresh and attention-grabbing.

This is positive PR. It is not damage control PR. Instead, it is proactive, innovative marketing of the uniqueness you have built into your product or service.

As an innovator, position yourself as a resource to the writers or producers in and around your chosen category.

Related or breaking news will come up, and you are positioned as an expert. They will contact you, and you have another opportunity to tell your story in a fresh context.

This is not about press releases, it is about fresh conversation. The key here is a unique need your product or service is fulfilling.

The rest is easy. Be proactive. Someone may have a need to fill a void with your story.

## Anecdote: Advertising vs. PR: The Innovator's Choice

CFI became the largest independent provider of Personal Financial Planning in the U.S., significantly as a result of publicity. Our numerous NBC *Today Show* appearances and *Wall Street Journal* and *The New York Times* articles put CFI in the spotlight. We received thousands of pieces of mail, including letters from many Fortune 100 employees. It opened up our awareness of this corporate channel of distribution.

Eventually companies like P&G, IBM, American Can, and Chevron became our clients. If you can get into a reporter's or blogger's mind and figure out what he or she needs and then help, you will become a valuable resource. When you become a resource and position yourself as an expert, the business will come.

The PR we got for CFI eventually grabbed the attention of Price Waterhouse. While looking for our third round of venture capital to expand CFI, PW bought our company.

Good PR can can take many shapes. Back in 1981, the South Seas Plantation was a locally known resort on Captiva Island in Florida. The owners arranged for *Sports Illustrated* to shoot the cover of their Swimsuit Edition on their white sandy beach, which stretched into clear blue water, with supermodel Christie Brinkley. It put the plantation on the map, and today it's a global destination for winter vacationers.

In my family's summertime neighborhood on the Leelanau Peninsula, something very similar happened. In 2011, the Sleeping Bear Dunes National Park along the west coast of Michigan was voted "Most Beautiful Place in America" by the viewers of ABC's *Good Morning America*. Since then, record numbers of people have visited the region.

Positive, pro-active PR. A resource to the media. An innovator's delight.

# 32. Giving Innovatively

Is there an inherent inconsistency between *business* and *giving* or *doing social good*?

There are some important trends and business social mores that suggest the answer is less obvious than a generation ago.

Where does innovation fit?

Business not only sustains itself by operating profitably but also by serving its stakeholders. A stakeholder analysis is key as the stakeholders may include anyone from stockholders to employees. Unquestionably, social consciousness and ethics plays out in this analysis.

As younger generations enter business, there is an expanding capacity and need for innovation that addresses elements of *giving back* and *social good*.

It is magnified when considering global issues, developing countries, and their needs.

There is significant room for innovation in giving and doing social good. How can this be accomplished? How can it be sustained?

## Anecdote: Giving Innovatively

Increasingly, younger generations seem to be entering the business marketplace with a strong desire to give back to their communities or to somehow work toward greater social good. World issues are a growing focus as well. Many of my students have spent time and effort applying their innovative skills to help not-for-profit organizations and causes.

Newer companies are tapping into the innovative business of giving. Warby-Parker, for instance, will donate a pair of sunglasses to someone in need for every pair of glasses their customers purchase. According to their website, over one million people in 35 different countries have received glasses.

Victory Van is another example of a business innovatively helping others. Victory Van, in Virginia, used a pink moving van—the only one traversing the country—to raise money for cancer victims by donating 10% of the cost of a customer's move. It had a positive effect on the customer and benefitted the company.

Recently, there was a woman who became pregnant but was also diagnosed with cancer. She had to make the horrific decision to forgo chemo treatment, which might have saved or prolonged her life, in exchange for saving her baby. Sadly, she died only a few days before her scheduled birthing date, but the baby was taken by cesarean. Victory Van donated a sizable gift on her behalf to family members who would raise the baby and incur medical expenses.

Innovation can come in various packages. Try giving.

# 33. Marketing and Branding for Higher Value

Certain categories lend themselves to innovative marketing or branding beyond the basic function of the product or service.

With writing instruments, for example, the cost of the inks, ballpoint, and shaft are a few pennies. And yet innovative marketing can provide value and prestige for the owner ranging from Bic, Pentel, Paper Mate, Parker, Cross, or Mont Blanc.

Pricing can range from $.25 to over hundreds of dollars for a pen, yet the commodity writing capability is virtually the same.

Watches from Timex to Rolex all tell accurate time but comment differently on the wearer.

Costume jewelry versus the real thing.

A cup of coffee. Pennies per cup brewed at home. $2 to $4 brewed at Starbucks.

A filet at $28 or $50 depending on the experience.

A car at $18,000 versus $50,000? The commodity value of transportation is similar, but the prestige, or the way you feel about yourself, or the design aspects, can provide meaningful differentiation.

Psychological and emotional needs are real. They can be quite subtle. They require innovative thinking. And pricing.

## Anecdote: Marketing and Branding for Higher Value

For some, a pen is just a pen. It doesn't really matter what it looks like as long as it is able to write. For others, a pen is a status symbol.

The same goes for purses. A purse can hold all sorts of things like glasses, pens, wallets, and phones, but for some, a purse can be a status symbol and even an expression of who they are. Even though two similar looking purses might be made of high-quality leather, the one bearing a Coach, Chanel, Louis Vuitton, or Prada logo makes a much different statement than a purse with a lesser known emblem.

Remember when Swatch watches were popular? They became collectable because of their trendy designs yet told time no better (or worse) than other watches on the market. A Timex is a perfectly accurate watch, yet a Rolex will turn heads. But even if no one else notices the fancy watch, it can still make the wearer feel good. And now we have the Apple Watch.

Surprisingly, higher college education has become brand and pricing related. How superior is an ivy league education at $50,000 per year versus a state or public university at $10,000 to $20,000? What is the job and career payback for the investment of time and cost of the loan?

Look for innovation here in the years ahead.

Branding and design. Innovation. Pricing.

It all makes a difference. It adds value.

## ɔcal

ɑl is good.

ʔtic. It's personal. It's locally crafted. It's not shipped in. It's hand-written. It's fresh.

Often a brand name, even if well-recognized, means it was produced or grown somewhere else and shipped in.

That might be okay for bananas (since we can't grow them in most places in the United States), but for strawberries, corn, lettuce, or local arts and crafts, or even brews, local equals authentic and not mass produced.

There are more innovations around *local* to be observed and marketed.

## Anecdote: Be Local

*Buying local* is a growing trend in the U.S., although it is nothing new, really. In France or Italy, people have walked down to their local markets daily to buy fresh bread and vegetables for centuries.

With the near takeover of big box stores, some Americans long for that feeling of authenticity, and they see the effects of their smaller, closer-to-home businesses dying off. They notice the quality and longevity of the goods have changed.

Chains like McDonalds and Applebees have had a profound effect on the American diet, but eating what is grown in one's proverbial backyard is reshaping our food culture. Restaurants serving higher quality, fresher foods grown on local farms realize positive perceptions as well as financial benefits.

Brewers are tapping into the local movement as well. Lagunitas Brewing Co. has created a whole "local" marketing campaign and culture to promote its beer. While the big guys like Budweiser are not going away, more and more craft beers are featured at bars and restaurants—and many are preferred by customers. It goes back to supporting your family, friends, and neighbors—the people growing and producing what you need.

And now whiskey distillers, too. More local, more crafted. More expensive.

Quality. Authenticity. Local.

# 35. Identifying the Experience Continuum

When does an experience begin? Or end?

Is it when the food is served at a restaurant? Is it how the food is presented on the plate? Or, does the experience begin when you walk through the door and are greeted by the maitre de? Maybe the experience starts when you make your reservation or hand your car keys to the valet parking attendant.

Was your table visited by the chef? Were you called the next day to confirm your experience was satisfactory? Did you receive a coupon in the mail to encourage a repeat visit? All of these individual events fall within the experience continuum and are worth identifying and analyzing.

What about going to a movie: Is it the movie itself? The advance ticketing? Parking? The greeting? The comfort of a reclining easy chair? The sound system? The customization of the sound system (earphones)? The exit process?

Most services have a sequence of events and significant innovation can take place at various points along this continuum. Where are the satisfaction gaps?

Pull back to 30,000 feet. Look at the service and potential experience as an entire sequence innovatively.

When can it begin? When can it end?

## Anecdote: Identifying the Experience Continuum

When *does* an experience begin or end—and how does that experience affect the consumer?

There are car washes—and then there are *car washes*. At one, you pull into a damp, cement stall, drop your quarters into the box, twist a dial to the correct setting, and then scrub down and spray off your car. You might get tangled up in the hose and get your feet wet. In the end, this car wash is just fine—it does the job.

Or, you can go to a car wash that does everything for you while you wait and sip a complimentary coffee. You see, through the big glass windows, your car being shampooed and buffed like it was at a spa. Not a drop of water is left to mar the exterior, and you leave feeling pampered. $4 or $20? What is the experience worth (or not worth) to the consumer?

What about going to see a movie? Does the experience begin when you search Rottentomatoes.com for reviews? Or when you purchase the tickets and buy popcorn? Or when the movie finally begins after the previews? Or the special, easychair seating? When does the experience end? After the credits roll? When you leave the theater and get into your car? When you get home and write a review or discuss it with friends?

Think about a football game—is it kick-off to final whistle? Certainly tailgating is an American phenomenon. Or does the experience include entering the stadium, the halftime show, replays? Are you lucky enough to be in a stadium box with food, beverages, and protection from the elements? Was your parking close to the stadium? You might even enjoy an after-party.

What can make an experience more memorable? Worth paying extra for? When can it begin or end more innovatively?

# Organizational Effectiveness

# 36. Progressing in Career

One powerful way to imagine your career progression is by examining the "T" model. Notice that the progression is not only rising *up* but *across* as well.

Innovative minds, in today's complex global companies, often work effectively *across* functions and geographies after they have risen *up* within a "functional silo."

As one gains experiences across the organization, one gains integration skills and a network that enables him or her to lead differently. Work up and out of your silo. Innovate across functions, divisions, and geography. This can be especially powerful if across includes other countries as well.

Leaders and innovators and *integrators* of the future will work effectively *across* the organization.

## Anecdote: Progressing in Career

At the University of Virginia, Darden, my students often came to get their MBA partly due to their reputation in former jobs as *doers*—reliable, smart people who got things done. Many had to delegate tasks, direct others, and motivate small groups. This is where many of my students felt as though they were stuck—in sort of a silo—in their former jobs and were not progressing as fast as they would have liked.

At Darden, students would pick up broader management skills then see themselves working more effectively across an organization and integrating various aspects. A more logical career evolution might then be to apply their experience to other functional, divisional, or process areas, and ultimately for some, to countries outside the U.S. This type of career progression—up from the singular, functional silos and *across* the organization—produces meaningful results.

As early as the 1970s and 80s at Gillette, there was virtually no progression to top management if an employee did not have experience working overseas and across multiple functions. In smaller operations outside of the U.S., one was exposed to many functional areas and was not trapped in a silo in one area.

In Singapore or France for example, a leader might be responsible for sales, but also be involved in logistics, currency, government relations, public relations, human resources, and many other areas. Given the early international aspects of the shaving business, over half of the Gillette Board of Directors in the mid 90s held a foreign passport.

Working *across* in today's smaller and technologically connected world is increasingly important to innovative career development.

# 37. Being Transparent and Open

A culture shift to innovation may cause a significant change in the need for transparency and openness.

Change can cause some people to resist. To dig in. To protect! Change can mean perceived loss of control and power.

Recognizing this is one key dimension of senior leadership. The new and innovative leaders must be empowered. The old must be persuaded, retrained, and given an opportunity to participate. Information and goals must be shared.

Sometimes counterproductive or destructive behavior needs to be recognized and called out. It is unacceptable. In some instances, it may require a more severe reprimand for acute resistors. Most people will know who they are.

Transparency and the vision for innovative leadership is key.

New innovative leaders need high level support from the senior executives desiring change.

## Anecdote: Being Transparent and Open

Price Waterhouse had a 150 year successful tradition as a professional British audit organization serving large Fortune 500 clients. The clients had historically called Price Waterhouse when they needed services, and it was considered too aggressive (almost ungentlemanly) for a partner to call and solicit business.

As competition intensified, clients stopped calling and went elsewhere because they had been solicited by other companies with intriguing ideas. This global expansion of clients was just beginning.

The culture needed to change. Audit partners who had historically enjoyed multiple five to 10 year relationships were protective of their clients. They were not open or transparent about their relationships with senior client officers, and many audit partners were suspicious of other services the firm might sell that could ruin their annuity stream of business.

A new role, the Client Service Partner, was created. This partner would oversee all senior executive relationships across lines of service and multi-country quality control. This partner would also insure that client needs were being met by truly understanding the business, listening for emerging needs, and bringing in appropriate firm-wide experts.

This was a major cultural shift. Many partners saw the need for the new initiative, and their business flourished. Some of the more protective audit partners dug in and became gatekeepers. Many of their opportunities were lost to competitors who more aggressively sought to fill the needs of their clients. Many adapted, but a portion did not. They had to be reprimanded, and in extreme situations, they were asked to leave the partnership.

Openness, transparency, and solving client business problems became the new culture, and this led to decades of global growth.

# 38. Diversifying Teams

We each have our strengths, experiences, and points of view. We also have our beliefs and assumptions, and sometimes, unknown biases.

A diverse team helps us innovate. A diverse team also helps us observe things we don't easily see or see what we might have missed.

Diversity comes in some less obvious ways such as different functional skills. Analytical versus free associative skills. Different industry or category backgrounds. Diverse countries and economic or educational backgrounds. And of course ethnicity, religion, and language.

Think about your own skills and strengths. Be objective.

A successful innovator often surrounds him or herself with diverse team members.

Think about using a virtual team if not all skills are available in-house. Technology, periodic in-person meetings, and other communication techniques can supplement full-time team members.

Embrace diverse team members.

## Anecdote: Diversifying Teams

PricewaterhouseCoopers came to realize it needed to diversify its client teams well beyond focusing primarily on auditing. It started to focus on strategy and software consulting, international tax, benefits, financial planning, valuation, post-merger integration, dispute analysis, and coordination across multi-country engagements—just to name a few.

Diverse client teams for the larger, more complex client companies often had several hundred team members. This diversity with well coordinated leadership across functions, technical strengths, and countries became a competitive advantage versus the more "siloed" competition.

As client complexities of the business changed so did the need for diverse teams to satisfy these globally-coordinated teams. Diversity became part of innovation.

Similarly in the moving business, Victory Van benefitted from developing a diverse team when it realized it needed a mix of marketing, operations, and finance. It could not succeed without consistent attention to operations since this was its assurance of quality and repeat client business.

It wasn't just enough to sell their product, so innovation within operations led to add-on business opportunities with employees and moving crews on the job. These employees are now owners after instituting an Employee Stock Ownership Plan (ESOP), which was innovated with financial insights.

Encourage diverse teams. Reward them.

# 39. Sustaining Innovation: The Learning Organization

Successful, innovative companies and organizations never stop learning. They focus on customers.

They have their beliefs or knowledge (K). Then they learn (L) as their company grows and changes. And the customer grows and changes along with expectations. It is a continual process.

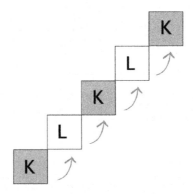

Sustaining innovation requires continued learning and re-shaping and experimentation with your customer—and not just the front end or customer-facing employees.

How to bring it back into the entire organization?

Continuous learning. Building on the knowledge and improved learning—this becomes the basis of sustaining innovation.

## Anecdote: Sustaining Innovation: The Learning Organization

Successful learning organizations like Amazon, Google, and Apple continually learn and apply new knowledge to growth. Some that have, at one time or another, stopped learning include Kodak, Polaroid, and several U.S. car manufacturers.

Learning organizations do not always get it completely right the first time. They get it close, take action, and then go to market. They learn from customer feedback.

Amazon, for example, diversified from books into many online products and services. By carefully listening and learning innovatively from customers and sophisticated measuring devices, they have responded with new innovative services to meet consumer needs. Their knowledge is the process of measurement, listening, and having an openness to change.

Apple learned innovatively from each generation of iPhones. New features are continually added while other features are de-emphasized as they gather feedback and knowledge. Who could have imagined that Apple would be a leader in telephones, cameras, email, texting, and voice recognition?

Google stresses innovation at each employee's level. They have an experimental mentality that encourages venturesomeness. Learning from success and failure is an expectation and deeply rooted in their culture. Part of their knowledge is the process of innovation—sustaining and encouraging an innovative culture.

Innovative companies are sustainable companies. It takes a *learning and knowledge* culture, and a focus on changing customer needs, to stay fresh and build upon what it has learned. This can be humbling as an organization cannot rest on its laurels. Innovators are always learning.

# ...ising 1/3; 1/3; 1/3

﹜ be an incredible observed phenomenon.

people in most organizations are ready to change, especially when adversity looms and is clearly identified. These are the early adopters—the agents of change.

1/3 will be slow to adopt change. They will follow the early adopters and change agents. They are important in the long term.

1/3 of an organization will resist change. These people live in the past—the "good old days," and these are the "turf protectors."

Instilling an innovative culture often creates stress and resistance to change. Start with the early adopters and agents of change. Often these are the leaders closest to the customer and can think like the client or customer. They are team players.

Who thinks like a client or a customer? Start here. Create success in sharing and celebrate positive, client and customer-oriented behavior.

Start with successes with the 1/3 early adopters. The next 1/3 will follow that success and those who made it. Sing their praises and compensate them appropriately.

For the 1/3 resistors, there may be a need for occasional "strong medicine" to combat blatantly negative behavior to signal that the organization is serious about change.

But, focus on the positive 1/3. Build client/customer success stories.

## Anecdote: Appraising 1/3; 1/3; 1/3

As PwC transformed from an audit firm in the 1990s to a global, multi-service line firm by the early 2000s, it encountered the "1/3, 1/3, 1/3" phenomenon.

The tax and consulting partners were among the first 1/3 to take on a change in leadership role. These were competitive businesses and the competition, globally, was heating up. Not everyone joined in, but there was a significant 1/3 group of partners sufficient to alter the culture. These were the partners who could feel the competitive "burning platform" and need for change.

Many, not all, of the audit partners were among the last 1/3 to change. They had been steeped in the historical success of an annuity business and could not easily accept the change taking place.

Firm leaders identified the first 1/3 more likely to change and raised them up by crediting them in internal communications and celebrating their client successes. Client success stories began to permeate the culture, and the leaders of these successes were publicly recognized.

The firm recognized not everyone would buy into the new culture immediately, so they focused most of their attention on the 1/3 who innovated with success in the new environment. It celebrated the 1/3 who were changing, and quietly reprimanded and financially de-incentivized the 1/3 who were slow or unwilling to change.

It is remarkable to note how applicable this phenomenon of 1/3, 1/3, 1/3 is across other companies—several of which we have observed in this book such as Gillette, PepsiCo, IBM, and GE.

# 41. Understanding Global Entrepreneurship

Corporations and partnerships have increasingly grown and sprawled across functions, divisions, countries, and processes.

Their customers and clients are likely experiencing many of the same trends concerning the same sprawl.

How can the "global central control" find *balance* for revenue and earnings growth across the organization? Doesn't this need to happen from the top down?

And yet, customer and client needs are often "localized" and need to be customized depending on location—especially in other countries. This requires service providers to be entrepreneurial, more spontaneous, more flexible, more independent, more innovative.

What is the right *balance* between the financial goals and measurements of "central control" versus the satisfaction of the local customer?

This balance requires an understanding and awareness of a new "global entrepreneurship."

It is causing many organizations to have a more horizontal structure. A flatter structure, allowing more authority at the local level. Many aspects of technology are facilitating this flatter, more innovative structure.

Global financial goals. Local and entrepreneurial customer needs fulfilled.

Global entrepreneurship.

# Anecdote: Understanding Global Entrepreneurship

In the early 90s, many US corporations like PepsiCo and its Pizza Hut division were eyeing potential growth in former communist block countries.

Several of us from Price Waterhouse met with the president of Pizza Hut Europe. After the meeting, we immediately called our PW office in Warsaw which had been in operation just two years.

To our surprise, the partner in charge of the office had recently hired a surveyor, and recommended that we perform a survey and research several properties near the location Pizza Hut was targeting.

*A surveyor on the staff of an accounting firm?* What did he know locally that we had not a clue?

Under communist rule, the government owned most of the property. But since the break up, enterprising (albeit dishonest) business opportunists assumed the property, yet had no legal rights to it. This information was just coming to the surface and needed to be sorted out.

The local PW partner could see these disasters coming, so he hired a surveyor to document and research the properties being considered by U.S. multinationals. It saved Pizza Hut two false starts, saved millions of dollars, and gave them nearly a year in important competitive advantages.

So for Price Waterhouse and PepsiCo's Pizza Hut, we see a strong example of global entrepreneurship. This relationship filled global needs for expansion but used strong local knowledge of former communist country practices.

Global entrepreneurship. A new kind of innovation.

# 42. Contracting Innovatively

All organizations (large and small) contract with outsiders. It is a way of life. A necessity. How can you contract innovatively with customers and suppliers?

Sometimes we hear or observe an idea that is so simple that it is innovative in its simplicity.

The concept of contract negotiations lends itself to this simplicity.

How to make a contract negotiation more of a win-win and less of a win-lose, which it often tends to be?

Think of this concept in these simple terms:

Agree with your client that there are three variables open for discussion. The client gets to pick any two of the three, and you get to deal with the third.

Here are the three variables:

- scope ( e.g., the range of services),
- timing, and
- price.

Think about this. Play with the variables on your next contract or price negotiation.

We've observed that it is often an innovative way to get to a win-win. Sometimes it is surprisingly simple.

## Anecdote: Contracting Innovatively

Sometimes the complex art of contracting or price negotiating can be simplified and innovated in different ways.

In our early days at CFI, we were often dealing with Fortune 100 companies who were notoriously tough negotiators. But we were also recognized as early stage entrepreneurial and unique in the market place.

We had one large company who was quietly considering a large downsizing of many thousands of employees. They wanted an extensive number of personalized financial planning reports for each employee done in a record compressed timeframe. Plus seminars. Plus an 800 number to field questions.

These brought out the three variables: *scope, timing,* and *price.*

We laid these out to be a win-win. They were unwilling to compromise on the timing—it needed to happen quickly. They were further convinced that the quality of service their employees were used to expecting necessitated in-person seminars *and* the 800 number employees could call at any time for help.

That left pricing. We priced it to cover our costs and make a modest profit. We turned ourselves inside out—but it was worth it. And it was profitable. It helped put us further on the map with other Fortune 100 companies.

Think of innovating with three variables in contracting. Sometimes simple is most innovative.

# 43. Accessing the Organization—Up and Down

Access to the highest levels *within* an organization for internal innovators is key. It works both ways. The top executive leaders need to know what innovations are coming up in the organization and reinforce the risk-taking of innovators.

The innovators need more than a miner's headlamp in the trenches, and they must have an opportunity to share their customers' findings.

Try for new access in informal ways if not formal.

Know that the top executives must have new, internally generated products and services for growing revenues.

Your success from the middle is their success at the highest levels.

## Anecdote: Accessing the Organization—Up and Down

In the early 1990s, the senior leadership team at Price Waterhouse saw the need for an innovative change in its organizational structure to deal with its changing global client needs.

It identified a small, select group of partners as part of an experiment to work across all internal service lines and countries around the globe since this would facilitate working more seamlessly with expanding client needs. These partners were given support as well as full backing to overcome any internal resistance or territorial behavior anticipated in a historically decentralized organizational structure.

These initial experiments were met with great success—in part, as a result of support and quick feedback derived from working up and down the organization. This access allowed fast resolution of conflicts using both the power of reason and in some instances, the power of measurement and compensation for uncooperative partners or locations.

As a result of these initiatives, Price Waterhouse became one of the most integrated global firms, and it boosted global client relationships and revenues as a direct consequence.

Listening is an important source of strategic information—and a morale builder for those on the front lines. But they need air cover.

Most complex organizations can benefit from the intelligent and tactful use of "access up and down the organization."

## 44. Building Trust Within the Company

Building trust is perhaps, at first, a strange characteristic of successful innovation.

Building trust is a balance of enthusiasm and positive outlook for new ideas and concepts. At the right time, after investigation, it is also the ability to see the pros and cons of an idea or project.

Know when to breathe life into a project and when to kill it and work on more promising priority projects. There is a bit of schizophrenia in sustainable innovators. Giving birth. When to end a project.

Build trust with your peers and collaborative team members. Building trust with your senior executives and your lower level team members is critical.

Build trust and candor with your customers. Working collaboratively with customers on their important priorities and future strategies is a gift. They must trust you to share their future.

Trust and objectivity. Breathing life. Ending. A delicate balance of "can do" and "can't do."

## Anecdote: Building Trust Within the Company

Gillette was considering entering the U.S. sunglass business and wanted to build on their sales, distribution, and merchandising strengths. They were evaluating an Australian sunglass company that was the category leader in Australia at the time that had a patented polarized lens.

Gillette chose an executive with a toiletry and cosmetic background to evaluate the acquisition. His approach was to take an objective pros and cons strategic examination of the category while maintaining his trusted reputation for acquisition evaluations.

After a lengthy evaluation, including the study of the dominant Foster Grant company in the U.S. market, the executive took an innovative step. With the help of a senior sales executive's referral from Gillette, he would quietly go into a local store with a supply of the Australian sunglasses and personally observe and sell sunglasses for a week. His findings were remarkable.

Very few potential customers paid attention to the polarized lens. In fact, the only serious potential customers for this line of sunglasses first picked them up and looked at themselves in the mirror before further considering purchase.

This confirmed what the executive had been witnessing in his research: it was often a cosmetic purchase. Customers commented that the glasses looked "10 or 15 years behind the times." Even if the lens was polarized, it did not provide any significant differentiation, and very few sunglasses in this proposed acquisition line actually sold.

The final recommendation was to pass on the acquisition. The executive's objective study and trust was reinforced by his innovatively spending time selling and observing the actual retail and consumer purchase behavior.

Trust fosters innovation.

# 45. Crediting

Successful innovation almost always requires collaborative teamwork, internal like-minded resources, and often external resources as well.

Team members, especially on higher-risk projects, desire and are often motivated by recognition. Crediting.

Credit them for their ideas, their actions, and their initiative. Further encourage objective pros and cons analysis. Credit them for taking risks.

Innovation is tough and often high risk. Find authentic ways of crediting your team members. Remember their contributions—verbally, and in writing.

Team players don't just "talk team"; they act it out—they credit others.

Often.

## Anecdote: Crediting

When Price Waterhouse acquired our Consumer Financial Institute (CFI) in 1986, IBM quietly confided to us they were considering a large downsizing. This would be the first time in modern history that they considered such a major workforce reduction after years of an informal "employment for life" social contract.

We had the opportunity to combine our CFI personal, artificial intelligence financial report for each employee at IBM and then conduct a series of in-depth seminars around the U.S. It was an unprecedented, massive program and represented one of the largest programs in such a narrow time frame in Price Waterhouse's history. All of the planning was strictly confidential given its unprecedented scale and the potential impact on IBM's financial markets.

The program went off without a hitch. As a newly acquired company, there was considerable trust, sharing, and exposure given the sensitive nature of the project. There was very strong crediting among the immediate team members from both organizations as the program unfolded. There were people who prepared a customized report for each IBM employee and a team of nearly 100 people who were trained to present employee seminars and answer timely questions.

The crediting and *esprit de corps* energized the team, and as it reached completion, it was lauded as an unprecedented initiative. It was also recognized as symbiotic—neither organization could have conducted these various components alone successfully.

The crediting expanded outside of IBM and Price Waterhouse, and soon a number of other Fortune 100 companies facing downsizing were added to the client list. Later, Chevron executives indicated this culture of "crediting and teaming" was an important part of their decision to hire the newly formed PW–CFI team.

Success has many fathers. Generous crediting cements a team. There are plenty of credits to go around.

# 46. Learning From Failures

Strangely enough, failures are a good thing when it comes to innovation.

There are two important perspectives.

First, if one is not pushing for uniqueness, then there is not a sufficient stretch. Pushing for something *different* involves risk—and therefore potential failure.

Second, it's important to learn from failures. Do an objective, in-depth pros and cons analysis. Probe yourself and others close to the project. There might be more than one reason for a failure. Dissect those reasons.

No one with significant career time around innovation avoids failure.

Learn from failure. You become a better, more experienced innovator.

It's not only okay—it is expected.

Learn.

Try again.

## Anecdote: Learning From Failures

Noxell Corporation (a.k.a. Noxema, now a division of P&G) took two new products to the test market. The first was a disinfectant spray that killed germs on contact. It was a very powerful germicide, and the advertising tagline was "Staffene Cleans the Unseen." The second new product was an effective "cucumber" anti-perspirant. There was a smile behind its advertising tagline: "It keeps you as cool as a cucumber."

Both product ideas had been created by two different leading New York advertising agencies. They were certain to have immediate success in these two large consumer product categories, both of which were dominated by Lysol and Right Guard, respectively.

The sell into the trade went very well, and the products were stacked on retailers' end aisles in specific test market cities when the advertising for these products broke. But a month into the advertising blitz, neither product moved. The end aisle displays were still there, virtually untouched, in all of the test market cities.

Staffene and the cucumber anti-perspirant flopped.

What happened? Why these failures? How could two different products in two different categories—both cleverly advertised with the help of large media budgets—be off to such a slow start? *Neither had a real product or perceived uniqueness that was meaningful.*

Lysol was already known to reliably kill germs. And cucumber? All aerosols felt "cool" when applied to the skin, and there was no other meaningful uniqueness or difference. Sometimes clever or memorable advertising is not enough. If a product claims to be like the current brand leader, but is not unique to the consumer, there is almost certain failure.

This should not be chalked up to a bad experience. Learn that "meaningful uniqueness" is key.

Don't make the same mistake again! Make it part of the organizational learning.

## 47. Maximizing the Power of One

The balance of power between a company and key customers seems to ebb and flow.

Sometimes, there is complex tension and a trade off of product, service levels, and pricing.

But, when the provider of *product* or *service* adds up the revenue across all of the divisions and all of the countries with all the same customers, this can lead to significant clout.

This clout can lead to an innovative opportunity to work with a customer in a partnering way. It can lead to access to senior officer relationships and across organizational creativity.

Add up the pieces. The sum of the parts may lead to a greater whole.

Unlock the innovation opportunities enabled by the power of acting as ONE. It can surpass the advantages of acting as decentralized divisions, practice areas, or entities.

## Anecdote: Maximizing the Power of One

PepsiCo had been dealing with a trend whereby large retailers (Walmart, CVS, and Kroger, for example) were flexing their muscles and demanding greater services and compensation for carrying and featuring their products.

Historically, PepsiCo had been intentionally decentralized by division, and there was healthy competition among divisions and executives. There was also a legendary competitive spirit with its top competitor, Coca-Cola.

This was the backdrop when PepsiCo began a more aggressive acquisition campaign to diversify and assemble product lines like Tropicana, Quaker, and Lipton tea.

But as Walmart, for example, began to increase demands across divisions for everything ranging from financial terms and coordination of truck delivery schedules at Walmart distribution sites, divisional autonomy began to change.

Top PepsiCo management requested an analysis. If they added up all the business across all the divisions of the company, PepsiCo *combined* was one of the largest, if not *the* largest provider of product dollars to Walmart—and most of their products were high turnover dollar volume.

This evolution and discovery (due to its new acquisitions) indicated PepsiCo's historically decentralized divisional approach required serious innovation. This evolved into its new concept—the Power of One.

The Power of One in the U.S., and then across other countries, led to an innovative, organization structural change that emphasized focus on customers, and with that, consequent innovations in measurement and compensation followed.

Acting as ONE can unlock innovation.

# 48. Building Trust With a Client

Establishing TRUST with a client is more than a word or gesture. It is very difficult to innovate with a client if there is not trust.

Trust is at the basis of any long term relationship. Are you to be a true business advisor?

Trust is often built during difficult times. Candor is key. Objectivity. Listening.

It often means accepting some financial hardship if the client is right and reasonable.

It certainly means not selling clients something they don't really need—despite end of the month financial pressures or broader, short-term Wall Street pressures.

Sometimes it requires candid feedback to the client on their own shortcomings. Their errors. Something they've missed or overlooked.

Candid give-and-take helps build objective, unemotional dialogue. This can lead to a balanced resolution of conflict.

Trust goes a long way. It's essential to a long-term relationship.

Trust grows out of a multidimensional, connected relationship.

It's where innovation starts.

## Anecdote: Building Trust With a Client

General Electric was one of the early U.S. corporations to re-enter Hungary in the post-Russian dominance period. In their exploration of various entry strategies, they decided to acquire Tungsram, Hungary's major lighting manufacturer.

In the process of providing business advice, and doing its due diligence work on this acquisition, the Price Waterhouse partners on the project established a trusted relationship with GE's senior management. The trusted team uncovered and shared a variety of issues that led to improved GE–Tungsram negotiations and better business value to GE.

At the project's conclusion, international leaders from both companies gathered for an intimate dinner at GE headquarters to celebrate the success and mutual respect and trust that had evolved during the project. What might be the next area of innovation?

Impressed by the global coordination and business insights from the PW team, GE confided that they would be aggressively opening operations in India, China, and Mexico. This information was so confidential that it had not been shared with any other advisors. It reflected GE's considerable trust in our team.

As a result of this exchange, we at PW began quietly visiting and setting up teams in India, China, and Mexico well in advance of any GE announcements. About six months later, and on the cover of Fortune magazine, GE announced it would be starting these initiatives.

TRUST with a client is key. Candid sharing. Good fun. A fast response to urgent needs, paired with good value and quality of services provided, equates to long term, trusted relationships.

Innovation starts with trust.

# 49. Putting the Client in the Middle

Most companies manage revenue and profits by divisions, countries, or lines of business. Few measure ongoing revenue and profit growth by client or customer.

How can we put the client in "the middle?"

For example, a top accounting firm

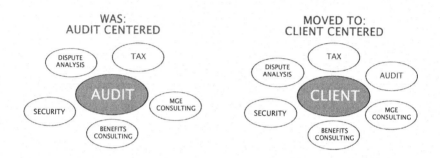

In moving to a *client-centered* organization and culture, the firm evolved from an audit-centric, controlled client to a business person (client service partner) capable of leading *all* service lines on a *global* basis.

Similarly, a leading global advertising agency went from an *advertising-centric* to a *client-centered* agency with media, market research, public relations, and other services internationally more equitably represented to the client.

Put the client in the middle.

Culture will change. Innovation follows.

## Anecdote: Putting the Client in the Middle

Price Waterhouse began as an audit firm over 150 years ago in England. It gradually added tax expertise as clients demanded it in the U.S. And in the 1970s, it began its serious focus on consulting services. But, Price Waterhouse's heritage and culture essentially centered around auditing. Senior management, and most of the firm's promotional materials, proudly stated that they had "100 of the Fortune 500" in the 90s.

Around that same time, an experiment had been underway to attract and secure non-audit clients to the firm. The term "client" was re-defined as "any company that paid the firm for any services rendered," and it had been discovered that, in addition to auditing, Price Waterhouse provided other services for over 450 of the Fortune 500 somewhere in the world.

As these experiments gathered momentum and included prominent companies like PepsiCo, Gillette, GE, and others around the world, a new philosophy emerged: "Put the client in the middle."

Global Client Service Partners led these client relationships and focused on the business needs of the client—not the firm's offerings. This new client-centered group had gone global and included nearly 100 clients. It included all lines of service and had become the model for successfully integrating a global, professional service firm.

The success of this new model provided enormous global growth and profits for Price Waterhouse and ultimately set the stage for the merger and integration with Coopers & Lybrand in to PricewaterhouseCoopers.

Put the client in the middle. When done successfully, it can transform an organization from a "selling culture" to a "need-fulfillment culture." When a client's needs are met, strong, successful relationships are formed.

Innovating with the client. Put their business needs in the middle.

# 50. Setting Priorities—New vs. Existing Products. Who Wins?

Sad but true. The "here and now" almost always takes priority.

If your desire is to get new products or services to the marketplace, you need someone (or a specific group) solely dedicated to that task.

Growing the revenue and profits of an existing business almost always wins the priority challenge.

Unfortunately, innovation often takes a back seat. It shouldn't.

Instead, put innovation in the front seat.

Better yet, let innovation do some driving. Don't muddy it with the existing "here and now" business.

## Anecdote: Setting Priorities—New vs. Existing Products. Who Wins?

One of the truisms of business is the need to separate out, organizationally, the focus on developing new products and services from maintaining existing products and services in an organization.

For entrepreneurs, new development is their primary—sometimes only—focus. It reflects their need for survival. Getting something new to the market place to begin a revenue stream is their driving force.

Larger organizations such as Gillette, PepsiCo, Pricewaterhouse-Coopers, IBM, and Procter & Gamble have capitalized on making this organizational separation between new and existing products and services.

But the list of organizations who do not separate out new product and service innovation is even longer. They, predominantly, do not experience innovative success.

Innovation is hard. It takes time and creative thought. It takes an experimental philosophy and willingness to take risks and endure failures. And to learn from those failures.

Not everyone is willing to do this. Find or recruit those who are willing and give them air cover and high level access.

Give them enough organizational separation, so they are not bogged down by day-to-day business and the pressures of near-term profits.

Innovation takes a degree of separation from existing business.

# Personal Strategies

# 51. Invest in Yourself

Every one of us has unique strengths, skills, and passions. Can you think about and list some of your own?

Then, take some time to hone your strengths, skills, and passions—whether at home or at work. Break down "next steps" so you can comfortably experiment and move them along.

This is an investment of time. It can also be an investment of money. But think about it: Ultimately it is an investment in yourself, your interests, and your passions ... not some impersonal marketplace or stock market.

It is totally within your control.

It could become your favorite hobby. It could become your career and passion.

Invest in yourself. It's your personal 401(k).

## Anecdote: Invest in Yourself

Seventy-year-old Bill Reed, an accomplished businessman and golfer, is passionate about old hickory golf clubs and the history behind them. In 2014, he and his collection of 40 sets of stunning, playable old hickory clubs were  featured at the 100th anniversary celebration of  the Leland Country Club in Leland, MI.

Bill found a way to get paid for what he is passionate about by turning his hobby into a retirement career. He now travels the country sharing his love of golf and the hickory club.

Bill is an inviting fellow with a white beard and decked out in his Scottish golfing hat, knickers, proper tie, and broad smile.

I caught him aside and asked him how things were going in this phase of life as we looked out over the course and gorgeous view of the surrounding lake. "Well George, you tell me. I played your 100-year-old course the last two days with my favorite set of hickories; today I'm meeting and talking with many of your members decked out in period costume; and next week I'm attending another club's 75th anniversary in the Colorado foothills." He then paused and with a wry smile said, "And I'm getting paid to do what I love best. Pinch me."

One important aspect of Bill's story, and many other stories, is that most of us have passions that we can experiment with early in life and "let it out" later in life.

For those who choose, it can often produce income and produce a return on investment.

Invest in yourself. Start early. Experiment.

## 52. Being Extra-Ordinary

Some of us are okay with just being "good enough" while others want to be *extraordinary*.

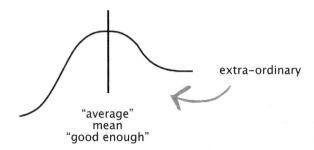

Think about the word "extra-ordinary."

What are your strengths and passions?

What is going around you? What are the innovative trends into the future?

You can be extra-ordinary if you experiment and find the places and niches that allow you to excel. Be passionate about your work, and innovate.

## Anecdote: Being Extra-Ordinary

I would often ask my students at Darden, "Would you rather be ordinary, or would you rather be extra-ordinary?" Most everyone in class would say *extra-ordinary*, of course, but most people actually fall into the *ordinary* range.

What would it take for you to be extra-ordinary?

For most of us, the power to become "extra-ordinary" means following our passion. It takes self-reflection to identify what that means for each of us, and of course it will be different for each of us.

It then takes further reflection and experimentation to determine what we are truly good at and what we really like to do. One of the observations we made over the years coaching the IBM and PricewaterhouseCoopers' executives is that it takes many replications and iterations to fine tune this.

Similarly, with my 30-something-year-old students, we could get them started thinking about being extra-ordinary, but it often took years (and plenty of feedback) before they could truly recognize the extra-ordinary in themselves.

So becoming extraordinary is not a quick fix. Instead, it's a fine tuning and longer term objective.

Imagine Steve Jobs thinking about being extra-ordinary.

Think of someone successful who you envy or respect. Talk to them. How did they go through this process?

Listen. Think. Imagine. Do you really want to be extra-ordinary?

## 53. Stretching Yourself

How often do you really stretch yourself, mentally?

Most of us stay in our mental comfort zone. It is comfortable and safe.

Experiment by taking yourself outside of your comfort zone. Speaking up in a group? Being quiet and listening? Each of us has different comfort zones. Identify these for yourself and practice them.

Often the greatest learning takes place as you stretch your comfort zone. Some call this the "yikes zone."

For many of us, this leads to exposing ourselves and to creative and innovative risk-taking. Coming up with ideas. Exposing the ideas.

Find diverse yet comfortable people to experiment with.

Stretch yourself. Enter your own "yikes zone."

## Anecdote: Stretching Yourself

George Prince developed a problem-solving and innovation method called Synectics and founded the Synectics organization in Cambridge, MA. He focused on the characteristics of creativity that could be taught and practiced in groups and found ways to "stretch" people by literally taking their minds on "vacation"—as a group.

Prince would present a challenge, such as "how to get jets into outer space," and then pose questions ("how to deal with weightlessness?") to get participants thinking. Eventually, through these creative exercises, he was able to take people's minds "on vacation."

A lot of the ideas participants came up with were absurd, but Prince could capture the logical ideas, too, through this process of enumerating and making lists. *What do you **like** about this idea? What **don't** you like?*

When it came to products, the next generation of shaving products in this case, Prince engaged a group of people who had never worked together before, including myself. He drew us out of our shells. It worked.

Let's switch gears and head to the ski slopes. Jeff had arrived at the top of the ski lift, looked down the hill, and said, "Yikes, I don't think I can do this!" Then one of his buddies shot down through the rocks and disappeared around the turn. His other friend said, "Don't think about it any more, just do it—or you'll be left here by yourself." Poof. Jeff flew down the hill.

We all need a push at times. Once we make it to the bottom of the hill, the experience—and the learning and the confidence we gain from it—is unparalleled. We will never forget it. Don't be afraid to push yourself into the "yikes zone"—past what you would normally do on your own. This is likely to be your best learning.

Are you uncomfortable with certain situations or tasks? Afraid of them? Maybe you need accomplices to enter together? This is perfectly okay. Learn to love your "yikes zones" and push yourself. Innovation is close by.

## 54. Acting on Best Advice

Think about the best advice you have ever received.

Start a list.

Think of the advice you received this year. Over the last five years? 10 years? Different organizations you've worked in? Personal advice? Advice related to traveling in other countries? For dealing with different kinds of people?

Innovating is often making the best of something—not settling for the "okay" but pushing yourself to excellence. Being the expert.

How are you coming on your list? Keep thinking of situations or categories near and far. You can use a notebook and pen or a notes app on your smartphone. Keep that list with you and continue to add to it.

It is an iterative process—one idea will beget another.

Next time you have an innovative opportunity or challenge, think of your "best advice" list. Maybe there is something you can borrow from it  and transfer to your particular situation.

This juxtaposition can lead to further innovative thoughts.

## Anecdote: Acting on Best Advice

Some of the best advice I have ever received relates to my experience traveling to China. An American-educated Chinese Price Waterhouse partner of mine made two salient points: "Don't just show up as an American who thinks he has all the answers," and "Don't let them know when you are leaving."

If they know when you are leaving, the heart of your visit—the problems or solutions or propositions you want to address—won't come up until the night before you leave. It will be too late and probably won't be acceptable.

Americans tend to think they can use a schedule as a way to pressure a resolution in their favor, but the Chinese have patience and a lifetime to make a decision. They are not measured on the same short fuse as Americans.

Listen, be courteous guests in their country, and don't let them know when you have to leave: This was powerful, long lasting advice, which we used for the next seven business trips to China.

Bob Nichols, who was a Price Waterhouse partner in charge of the firm's largest global client, IBM, also gave me excellent advice related to working internationally: "If you have a problem, no matter where it is (especially if it is in a different country), get on a plane. And don't resolve to act until you have gone there and listened to ALL sides of the issue."

Bob knew that cultural issues and "saving face" could easily become magnified internationally on behalf of the client as well as by one's internal team. The client isn't always right. Same with the internal team.

Go there. Decide first hand. Especially internationally.

Good advice. Start your list. Add to it. Use it. Innovate.

# 55. Spending the Day—Effectively

There are only 24 hours in a day. If you are feeling constantly behind or left with work and personal things always open, try this:

Document your own personal pie chart on how you spend your time. An example below on an average day:

An example - 24 hours        You (actual) - Fill this in

 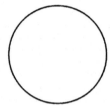

Now, how would you better like to spend your time in the future?

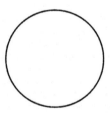

Track yourself. How are you doing after a few months? Over a year?

How much time do you allow for fresh, original thinking? Being creative? By yourself? With like-minded people?

## Anecdote: Spending the Day—Effectively

Getting the right balance in work and your personal life is one of the most difficult challenges innovative people face. And it changes depending on your enthusiasm for what you are working on and with your family situation.

While coaching several hundred IBM, PricewaterhouseCoopers, and other executives, we discovered that this was perhaps one of the most difficult challenges they faced.

Smart, highly motivated men and women who had a proven career track record struggled with time management. They were not devoting rigorous discipline and thinking to resolving this challenge—they were too busy attending to their daily activities. Many not sleeping well.

We went through a basic pie chart exercise that asked them to lay out their current 24 hour day, including sleep and "me" time. We then asked them to think about how they would *ideally* spend their 24 hour day. Putting that into a separate 24 hour pie chart was a challenge, but it opened their eyes.

One executive came up with a way to discover more hours in the day. He experimented with looking at email only every third day. He felt he had been wasting 1-2 hours a day on unimportant tasks. Two hours is 25% of an 8 hour day.

We worked with these executives over several months to have them self-evaluate their progress. For many, this was a highly revealing and motivating experience. Many reported they became happier and increasingly innovative and observant.

# 56. Thinking Innovatively—Where to Go

We are all very busy. There are daily emails and phone calls, and everything seems to be a priority requiring an immediate response.

So when do we make time to think creatively? What's the best place? It doesn't just happen. Innovation can get crowded out.

Think about your best think time. And *place*. While taking a shower? Morning or evening walk or run by yourself? On vacation? While driving?

Everyone is different.

What environment do you need to find or make to allow time and space for creative thinking?

Schedule a time for answering email or making calls. Determine your creative space to think by yourself.

Experiment. Make notes. Observe yourself over time.

Where is *your* best place to think creatively?

## *Anecdote: Thinking Innovatively—Where to Go*

Most of us are more innately creative than we give ourselves credit for. One of the challenges even the most creative people have is setting the time aside to focus on just that—being creative. And besides setting the time aside, finding the right place to further stimulate it.

Always write down your creative and innovative thoughts as you get them—don't wait and hope to remember them all.

Let me share a personal example. During my entrepreneurial days at the Consumer Financial Institute, we got hot on the media trail. These good fortunes led to a number of speaking opportunities around the U.S. and several overseas.

I was not a natural speech writer or presenter, so I evolved a method which eventually served me well. I would make bulleted notes after my shower.

Then, I took long walks down the beach in Scituate, MA. This became *my place*. The shoreline is rocky with interspersed sandy patches. It helped me think. Ideas would start to come together from earlier notes. I put a note pad and pen in my pocket (today I'd take my smartphone) and when a surprising, good connection came to me, I would write it down, so I wouldn't forget it.

Take your mind on "vacation" in a planned way, and let the power of random connections add to the sound bullets and logic already in place from earlier work. I found as I practiced this more frequently, I got better and better. Practiced innovation. It can work.

This happens best in iterations. Not all of the good stuff comes at once. Change and juxtapositions bring new connections that, in other circumstances, might seem quite illogical.

Find your right place(s). Let your brain do its thing.

# 57. Taking Action

Don't just think Big Thoughts—break an idea down into its parts.

Find a part that you can get started on.

Action leads to discovery, testing, and experimentation.

Get to marketplace learning, and get feedback from real people with the real need as soon as possible (first hand experience).

Listen to feedback and learn from it in order to make alterations.

It is active, repeated testing, experimentation, and end-user testing that leads to refinement and success. Stay out of the "ivory tower."

Execute. Experiment. Take action.

## Anecdote: Taking Action

Sometimes it is easier to focus on something that is immediate and needs to be decided on tomorrow or next week. But what about longer term opportunities?

Recently, we were faced with the prospect of rezoning a real estate parcel in Virginia. It was an important opportunity with a payoff eight to 12 years out, but we were told we had to act now, or the opportunity might pass us by.

How can we motivate interest in something that doesn't really bear fruit for 10 or more years? Here goes. With the help of several professionals who had great success in real estate, we identified the most likely steps over the 10 year period with benchmarks for progress. We then took the next 12 to 18 months to break down detailed actions and "next steps" to anticipate any turn of events as well as outcomes. This is *key*.

We then formed a team and budget to take the necessary steps and measured ourselves accordingly. Our small coalition included people with like-minded interests.

Today, we are nearly two years into this long-term project with high morale, active participation, and a "charged environment" team. We have gone from questioning our ability to sustain interest for such a long term project to being riveted on next steps and outcomes.

Take action. Break down long term into short term tasks that bring immediacy. Form a complementary team or like-minded group to share responsibilities and maintain momentum. All of these can help make it happen.

# 58. Experimenting

Find a way to go from the seed of an idea quickly to an experiment—preferably with the "end user."

Be out in the marketplace. Talk to real people (people who are ostensibly disinterested in your success but who ideally have a need for the product or service it fulfills).

In smaller or entrepreneurial companies, early experiments can be constructed at modest costs and manpower commitments. These are often the critical constraints.

In larger companies, experiments are more easily accepted versus more permanent changes. It gives top management early success stories to celebrate and build on. If an experiment is not successful, it can quietly go away.

Plan on a series of experiments and listen objectively to the reaction and results.

## Anecdote: Experimenting

In the early 90s, Price Waterhouse began an experiment to better manage the global relationships and business with its non-audit clients. It became clear that the firm had sizable pockets of business with many clients at various locations around the world, but these had grown up spontaneously, not through a strategic and organized effort.

Three companies were initially identified where there were some initial executive relationships but minimal business: Gillette, Pepsi-Co, and General Electric.

The initial hypotheses were that as the world was changing rapidly, there was a frontier of global growth opportunities to create a strategic thread of business innovation with these prestigious clients, and a few initial executive relationships could provide the seedbed of long term growth.

Another characteristic of these companies was that because they were non-audit clients, they did not receive a lot of attention in the firm and were under the radar for most of the dominant audit-centric partners.

The results of these initial experiments became legendary at Price Waterhouse and formed the basis of a total restructuring of the firm's largest non-audit clients. It grew to a varied industry array of 350 Fortune companies, globally—many of which became some of the largest clients of the firm. GE, for example, grew to a top 10 globally.

Quiet experimentation. Filling needs innovatively with senior executives. Following opportunities wherever it took Price Waterhouse in the world. Working seamlessly across boundaries like countries and lines of service. Celebration of success internally so that other partners would want to join in.

Innovative experimentation.

## 59. Making Bedside Notes

It's sad, but true: Making bedside notes can improve your sleep.

Most of us have experienced waking in the middle of the night with a brilliant idea or a solution to a problem.

Yet, when we wake up in the morning, the thought is either gone, or not as crisp.

When we sleep, part of our brain keeps working. It may make an unusual connection. It's on vacation.

Interestingly, by writing the essence of an idea down on a notepad or in a smartphone "notes" app, you can let go of the idea and go back to sleep.

Sleep better. Make your bedside notes, test them by the light of day, and then decide.

## Anecdote: Making Bedside Notes

For years I would wake in the middle of the night, have what seemed like a brilliant thought, but by morning it was forgotten. Or it didn't seem as brilliant as it was when I had it. I eventually started making notes. It helped me get back to sleep faster, and by dawn's light, I knew whether the thought was as innovative as I had hoped. It happened a lot.

One time in particular stands out. The stock market had a precipitous drop on Monday, October 19, 1987—the largest Dow Jones percentage drop to date in U.S. history. I had been on the Today Show a few times, and they seemed to like an easy to understand, straight-talk style. They called me to see if I could help "calm the American people." I said yes, outwardly confident.

I was with two colleagues when I hung up the phone. They said the color immediately left my face. *What was I going to say?* Immediate research, discussion, and innovative thinking. I discovered that, even with this precipitous one-day decline, the market was at about the same level it had been a year ago.

That night, I awoke several times in a near panic. *How could I possibly relax their viewers if I couldn't relax myself?* Back to sleep. It came to me. I got up and made some bedside notes. This could be it!

I was in the green room by 6:30 a.m., and the show started at 7:00. At 7:05, I was asked, "Mr. Barbee, what is the average person to do?"

"Well, the market is at approximately the same level it was a year ago. This is like the 'Rip Van Winkle effect'. If you had gone to sleep a year ago and just woke up this morning, the market would be at the same level. You can go back to sleep and relax. No reason to panic— just take a long term, multi-year view, and don't let daily fluctuations ruin your day."

Thanks to bedside notes, I got through the segment. Apparently they got a lot of mail with good comments. We got invited back.

# 60. Discovering the Mosaic

Sometimes true innovation is like creating a large mosaic but starting with the pieces and constructing outward and upward to the grand design.

It can be like starting with a pile of complex puzzle pieces but not having the box cover to guide you to the finished picture.

What questions can guide you through this messy, often awkward design phase and journey?

What is the fundamental need to be filled?

What dialogue can lead to clarifying the true unfulfilled need?

How will this concept be unique versus your competition's concept?

Constructing the mosaic and grand design of true innovation is a journey.

Experiment. Listen. Engage in dialogue.

Think of discovering the true mosaic, the grand design, as an exciting journey.

## Anecdote: Discovering the Mosaic

Many innovative products and services end up in very different places from where they started. Some from humble beginnings are barely recognizable in their final form.

When we founded the Consumer Financial Institute, financial planning was essentially a wealthy person's service. A number of companies provided financial planning to senior executives of large companies costing between five to 10 thousand dollars per year.

We thought there was a need to provide *objective* financial planning to middle income families. We went directly to the consumer and *did not sell* other financial products to avoid building in a natural bias for sales and ruin perceived credibility.

We got our break from some solid publicity, and the mosaic began to form. It was different than what we expected, but it was good.

For example, we heard from numerous Fortune 500 companies, not just individuals. From one Fortune 100 company, we had 10 different employee levels write to us including a senior officer, a mid level HR representative, people from sales, and a few financial department employees. We even heard from a few line workers.

This opened our eyes. We had hit an unexpected, positive nerve. Just as 401(k) accounts were becoming popular, employers wanted their employees to be objectively educated, self-reliant with their personal finances, and no longer solely dependent on their company.

Our business took an unexpected turn. The mosaic became increasingly clear. The real opportunity for CFI was providing financial planning to companies like Procter & Gamble, IBM, and Chevron for their employees—not directly to the consumer. Companies would pay for all or a significant portion of the cost.

Although it was not visible at the outset, a corporate channel of distribution opened up. The winning mosaic. Take the time to decipher it.

# 61. Being an Innovative Rainmaker

Ford Harding wrote a book called *Creating Rainmakers*. In it, he identified skills of senior business development leaders. The importance of these skills is that not only can they lead to successful revenue growth, but in my experience, that they lead to innovation with customers and clients as a means to that end.

We were inspired at PwC and IBM to adapt and revise these concepts. This was a new dimension to add innovation.

Let's take this further. Think about it. Revenue growth will almost certainly result by innovatively addressing and helping clients to self-discover their own true needs.

What are the most common characteristics of successful innovators/rainmakers?

What are your own personal characteristics and personal strengths?

Make a list of both before you go on.

| My own charactristics and personal strengths: | Characteristics of successful, innovative rainmakers: |
| --- | --- |
| | |
| | |
| | |
| | |
| | |
| | |

## Anecdote: Being an Innovative Rainmaker

How similar do you feel your strengths are compared to those of a rainmaker's? Here are some characteristics of successful rainmakers:

- They have no single personality type (i.e. introvert or extrovert).
- They are optimistic.
- They are highly motivated.
- They are persistent and resilient.
- They are good listeners and synthesizers.
- They are excellent networkers.
- They have a personal system to track and organize.
- They are disciplined.
- They believe "I" can make a difference.
- They are self-starters and team oriented.
- They push boundaries and break rules.

How do you compare yourself to their list?

How do you rate yourself as a business developer?

How close is the list to a successful innovator?

# 62. Assuring How You Want to Be Regarded

How often do you get to take time out to think about who you really are? Where you have been? Where you want to be in five years? For your own satisfaction? How do you want to be regarded by others? At home? At work?

Thinking like this can often be a journey. It doesn't happen overnight, and it can and will change.

Try it. Take notes and keep them, so you can refer back. Review your notes annually. Teach yourself.

This exercise and process is one of the keys to creativity and happiness. It is part of the balance that allows us to sustain a high level of productivity and creativity.

Where we are headed is directly in our control. In this process lies our true commitment to be more creative and innovative.

## Anecdote: Assuring How You Want to Be Regarded

Do you want to be regarded as an innovator? Will it be your own entrepreneurial business, or will you work innovatively for a small, medium, or large business?

Keep in mind that it's not a bad thing to learn on someone else's nickel. We can be creative, learn a lot about practical business aspects, and make substantial contributions to the organizations we choose to work for along the way.

I thought about how I wanted to be regarded in the future after we sold our entrepreneurial company, CFI, to Price Waterhouse. I had always wanted to be a global executive and travel the world to grow and innovate businesses.

In the early 90s, following the fall of the Berlin Wall and the Russian Revolution, the world was rapidly changing—including political and business landscapes. This was my opportunity.

I began using my network of business and personal friends and soon found that most of the Fortune 500 were trying to figure out how to take advantage of this monumental shift in the global business landscape.

After a few initial trips to Europe, Eastern Europe, and Asia, it became clear these companies were on the verge of rapid expansion internationally. This would be the next business innovation frontier in my judgement.

Being regarded as an international business leader was logical for me. It was quietly one of my life goals.

How do *you* want to be regarded? You can make it happen.

## 63. Finding Your Personal Genius

The closer to the intersection of what you "like" and what you are "good at" is your personal genius.

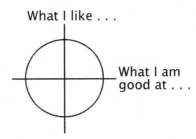

It is closer to where your passion is.

If pursued, an idea or concept for a product or service will be self-motivating, high energy, and sustainable over time.

It can be part of a life journey. Or it can happen surprisingly quickly.

The important thing is to give it thought. Quiet thought. Reflect.

Only you will know.

It's your *personal genius*.

## Anecdote: Finding Your Personal Genius

Finding your own precise intersection of "likes" and what you are "good at" is a journey, but a journey that has many payoffs and rewards.

I found some of the self-help books like *What Color is Your Parachute?* and *How to Get Control of Your Time and Your Life* to be helpful tools. How can you go wrong if you are pursuing what you like and what you are good at—all of which equals what you are passionate about?

I approached what I thought was a final fork in my career road. The Dean offered me an invitation to teach as the first faculty Batten Fellow at the University of Virginia Darden School of Business. I would have said "innovating with customers" was close to my own personal genius bull's-eye, and the school wanted to increase its graduate offerings and reputation in the innovation arena. So it looked like a fit.

I started reflecting on my business career and the various "nine lives" I had enjoyed as it progressed. What were the common threads that ran through it? It finally came to me: a broader definition of innovation and, more recently, with a global twist. This would become my course at the business school.

After 14 years of teaching, it was time to write a book on the subject that I am most passionate about—*innovation*. I had my teaching years experimenting and keeping pace with nearly 500 technology savvy students. I had an opportunity to reflect on my nearly 45 years of business experience. All this has broadened my definition of innovating well beyond the common definitions one hears in business.

So the journey continues for me.

How is your journey progressing? Aim for your intended bull's-eye. As a good archer or rifleman, you will seldom hit it without much practice, hard work, and experimentation.

Aim High. Stay with it. The process gets you closer to your real passion.

# Epilogue

## *How to Ensure a Winning Innovation*

Do you want to become more innovative? In products or services?

Are you stuck for the moment? Perhaps you have a personal "thinker's cramp" or are involved with a small group or large company and have "organization cramp."

Either way, feeling stuck can cause a negative attitude and contribute to lack of success.

Be sure to reflect on a few simple guidelines.

The following characteristics must (almost) always be met to be a sustainable success—whether it involves a new product, service, or experience:

- Is there a need—or a cleverly "imagined" need (such as a microwave, smartphone, or Facebook that truly raises the bar)?
- Can the product, service, or experience fill the need uniquely?
- Can it be communicated?
- Can it be profitable (medium to longer term)?

After writing this book and reading through the comments of my early reviewers, I came to realize that there is one additional personal characteristic of innovative leaders.

It's CURIOSITY.

Asking questions of others.

Asking questions of oneself.

A characteristic of an innovative leader is truly listening and being curious with authentic questions and probing. Searching for the new and different. Anticipating unfulfilled needs. In essence, it is helping people further their own thinking by asking questions.

# About the Author

## *Where it Started for Me. And the Possible Relevance for You.*

I hated my first job. It was all number crunching.

I wanted to be more innovative. I wanted to be more creative in my work and started to realize innovation and creativity are relative terms. Was I innovative? Was I creative? What would be the sign posts along the way to measure myself against?

We are often reluctant to express our innovative ideas or share them with others—particularly in a business environment where we are conscious of continually being measured, evaluated, and judged. And a business environment is one that does not typically encourage risk taking. In fact, taking risks is often frowned upon and sometimes results in punishment for being too venturesome or straying outside the established norm.

## *Innovation in Consumer Products: The Shaving Industry*

Then I got lucky. While still a confident "twenty-something," I landed a job with Wilkinson Sword, a British company that was on the verge of discovering a product that would revolutionize the shaving industry: the encapsulation of a stainless steel blade inside a disposable plastic holder. The geometry was now secure (and not variable as it had historically been for decades with the double-edged blade screwed down into the razor handle).

The attention in the industry going forward focused on the blade and geometry. Gillette and other companies followed suit and came out with two, then three, and now four fixed blades per shaver head. The benefit for the consumer was much less nicking and a quantum leap for the clean, close shave.

Introducing this revolution gave me a huge boost in business self-confidence. As my career progressed, I came to appreciate that many of my colleagues, peers, superiors, and direct reports were not as confident in innovation as they had every right to be. Many were adverse to taking risks and seemed to shun things that were new and different.

Along the way, I sought (and benefited from) other innovative entrepreneurs and new product development colleagues who showed me the ropes and further improved my learning, curiosity, and confidence in the "new and different."

## Financial Services Innovation

Following my years in the consumer goods industry, I became an entrepreneur and co-founded the Consumer Financial Institute (CFI). It became the largest independent provider of financial planning in the United States and revolutionized financial planning as well as that aspect of the financial services industry, which had historically catered only to wealthy individuals. Corporations like IBM, Procter & Gamble, American Can, Chevron, and other Fortune 500 companies used our services for educating their employees (most of whom were middle income) to become increasingly self-reliant financially.

The period of downsizing many Fortune 500 companies experienced in the 1980s and 90s underscored the need for average employees to become better managers of their finances. Also, at a time when 401Ks were becoming well established, the need for self-directed employee investments grew.

CFI became a dominant player and revolutionized the personal financial planning industry. Many insurance and brokerage leaders followed our lead, and PW ended up purchasing our company. This further boosted my confidence, and I realized that what I had learned while innovating products could also be transferred over to innovating in the *services* industry.

## Global Professional Services Innovation

With Price Waterhouse, I was given the global responsibility to reset a strategy to build the business of the firm's non-audit clients. We discovered that while the firm had 100 of the Fortune 500 as audit clients, there were another 350 Fortune customers who conducted other types of business with Price Waterhouse somewhere in the world.

In the 90s, when the world was dramatically changing following the fall of the Berlin Wall and the revolution in Russia, the climate was ripe for another type of revolution—doing business on an integrated, global basis that had never before been pioneered.

This led to enormous multi-billion dollar growth for Price Waterhouse with its global clients and helped set the stage for an eventual merger with Coopers and Lybrand in the late 90s (Pricewaterhouse-Coopers, now rebranded as PwC).

The cross-border client work contributed to the newly merged firm's Global Ambition and its recognition as one of the most *integrated* global organizations in the world.

## Innovation is Teachable and Learnable

While working in business innovation across products and services and then across countries and other boundaries, I continued to observe that many colleagues who were initially reluctant to let their creativity flow could be converted to innovators. It was contagious.

Top management and the leadership of our clients started believing in the power of innovative thinking. It was transformational, even if slower, in the rather staid industries like accounting and tax but a bit more quickly adapted in consulting.

In more recent years, I was brought back into PwC and IBM to help train and mentor the next generation of leaders to be increasingly effective at business development, innovation, and integration across silos internally—and with their clients. This experience, paired with teaching nearly 500 students at Darden School of Business, has given me further confidence and evidence that innovation skills *can be learned. Can be taught.*

Some individuals may be innately more creative and innovative. Yet, I have come to believe and witness that executives and students alike can learn how to innovate—far beyond how they perceived themselves. Far beyond how their superiors may have perceived them initially.

We all have the ability to innovate—we just need to be open to thinking differently, and learn how to reframe our observations and ideas in new ways.

*And then transfer them to new situations.*

Now I am curious about your reactions. This is a compilation of nuggets from a lifetime of practical experiences. I was also fortunate enough to be surrounded by men and women who shared a similar passion about the future, trends, and innovation.

What stories and situations have resonated with you? Are there several nuggets that are more impactful than others? Let's compare notes. Send me your comments. What additional nuggets of innovation have you discovered in your own work?

We are already working on the next volume of Innovation Nuggets, so I would sincerely welcome your thoughts in order to be more inclusive.

Please visit my website at www.InnovationNuggets.com to continue this conversation with me.

# Credits

As we have observed, innovation is a "WE" thing, not an "I" thing. The following people, publications, and companies have all played an important role in the inspiration for this book:

## *Individuals*

- Susan Carlson: editor and positive force; there for me in every step of the process and who brought me into the state of the art use of technology and provided many publishing insights.

- Jim Gilmore: co-teacher at Darden; co-author of *The Experience Economy* (updated in 2011) and Authenticity: What Consumers Really Want (2007). He inspired me, and we brainstormed around nuggets of experiences, gaps, renting, the continuums, and with his partner Joe Pine, "mass customization."

- Shanker Ramamurthy: fellow teacher at Darden; IBM Executive; co-author of *The Specialized Enterprise: A Fundamental Redesign of Firms and Industries* (2005). He inspired me around industry deconstruction and reconstruction nuggets.

- Robert Spekman: Professor Emeritus of Business Administration, University of Virginia Darden School of Business. He inspired me around leading from the middle and business-to-business nuggets.

- Alec Horniman: Professor of Ethics, Strategy and Leadership, University of Virginia Darden School of Business; a pioneer in ethics. He inspired me around the learning organization and extraordinary leaders nuggets.

- UVA Darden faculty including Elliott Weiss, James Clawson, R. Edward Freeman, Paul Farris, and Brandt Allen.

- Darden Dean Robert F. Bruner (appropriately named "Dean of the Decade"), Dean John Rosenblum (Darden visionary of the new campus, and close friend), Dean Ted Snyder, Dean Ray Smith, and Dean Bob Harris. And new Dean Scott Beardsley, 2015-Present.

- UVA's Batten Institute—over 60 Batten Fellows.

- Jeanne Liedtke: author of *Designing for Growth: A Design Thinking Tool Kit for Managers* (2011).

- John Colley: provided the opportunity to co-teach at Darden and teach about Thomas Jefferson in an historic pavilion on the UVA campus.

- Thomas Knowlton: previous President Kellogg North America, former Dean of Business Faculty at Ryerson University, and insightful reviewer.

- Tom O'Neill: former Global Leader of PwC Consulting Practice and insightful reviewer, friend, and respected leader over the merger of the consulting practice with IBM.

- Steve Momper: Director, Darden Business Publishing with publishing insights and early on reinforcements.

- John Sullivan: Darden Executive Ed colleague for his thoughtful, constructive, critical review of the entire manuscript in detail.

- Philippe Sommer: Director of the Center for Entrepreneurial Leadership and the i.Lab at UVA; Scott Snell leader of Darden's Exec Education; and Mike Lenox, leader of the Batten Institute of which I was honored to become its first Faculty Fellow of over 60 now so recognized.

- Sankaran Venkataraman ("Venkat"): Professor of Business Administration and Senior Associate Dean for Faculty and Research at the Darden School of Business; co-teacher and mentor.

- Nearly 500 bright, dedicated students and their observations of over 2000 companies (and best practice global companies) during our classes together at Darden. They have helped keep me current on innovations and in many instances, several years ahead of significant trends and developments like social media, "giving back," attitude trends, etc. In particular, Lia Davidson, who helped influence the re-write of my introduction.

- Dom Tarantino: PwC wisdom in the CFI merger and support for Global Client Partner role, Ken Sicchitano, Paul Weaver, Mark Lutchen, Tom O'Neill, John Barnsley, Bill Gilmour, Mike Goulden, Amal Ganguli (India), Kent Watson (China), Dennis Nally, Sr. (who perpetuated and expanded the Client Service Partner role and Channel II initiative), Tom Ruble (co-founder of Management Horizons, leading authority of the retail industry, and a co-author of a Price Waterhouse article on category management and customer relationship), Arthur Ho partner (Hong Kong), Graham Whitney for his insights on the "T" of career path progression, and the many hundreds of partners in our network.

- George Prince: founder of Synectics, and The Practice of Creativity (1970) and inspiration of brainstorming and the absurd idea nuggets.

- S. Brady Brown: former SVP William Esty Advertising and inspiration for four key elements of successful new products and other early on career insights.

- Kenneth Roman: former CEO of Ogilvy & Mather and inspiration for the nugget putting "the client in the middle."

- Jim Fitzpatrick: brilliant Wilkinson Sword British engineer who oversaw the Bonded Razor from development to market and who became a lifelong friend in the process.

- Jonno Hannifin, Jim Kochalka, Michael Kitson, Jack Dunleavy, and Nora Dunleavy (unrelated IBM executive), and other faculty of the Rainmaker Program for IBM and PwC. And Jonno for his articulation of stretch in the "yikes zone," and personal genius concepts.

- Tom McWilliams: friend, guest lecturer, and venture capitalist.

- Lee Fifer: close friend, advisor, and board member at Victory Van Corporation.

- And my book reviewers and researchers, chronologically, such as James Clawson, Steve Momper, John Sullivan, Debbie Quarles, Steve Peltzman, Shanker Ramamurthy, Tom O'Neill, Steve Reinemund, Tom Knowlton, Dennis Nally, Dean John Rosenblum, Dean Bob Bruner, James Gilmore, and Chrissine Rios, for their timely responses and constructive insights.

- Molly: my wife who put up with me and endured the writing of this book, an inspiration to me in her athleticism and art excellence. Also for her insights around white space and a meditative approach to the nuggets themselves. And her help with a number of visual ideas. And our four sons Gregory, John, Scott, and Jefferson with their reviewer insights.

## Books

- The Experience Economy (1998) by Jim Gilmore and Joe Pine and inspiration for "mass customization." nuggets.

- The World is Flat: A Brief History of the Twenty-First Century (2005) by Thomas Friedman and a number of inspirations around his 10 Flatners, Convergences, and Corporate Rules.

- Fish! Tales: Real-Life Stories to Help You Transform Your Workplace and Your Life (2002) by Stephen Lunden, Harry Paul, and John Christensen, and the FISH! video (the story of Seattle's Pike Place Fish Market); and their inspirations around Play, Make Someone's Day, Be There, and Choose Your Attitude.

- *What Color is Your Parachute?* (1970, revised each year since 1975) by Richard Bolles, which I read 20 times throughout my career; it inspired me to pursue and chart my innovative career.

- *How to Get Control of Your Time and Your Life* (1989) by Alan Lakein with insights to time management and balance and A, B, C priorities.

- *Creating Rainmakers: The Professional's Guide to Training Professionals to Attract New Clients* (2006) by Ford Harding with a direct inspiration to our Rainmaker Program at PwC and IBM and valuable insights to successful rainmaker characteristics and principles.

- *Creative Confidence: Unleashing the Creative Potential Within Us All* (2013) by Tom Kelley and David Kelley with recent reinforcement to taking action and belief in creative inspiration.

- *The Innovator's Dilemma: When New Technologies Cause Great Firms to Fail* (2011) by Clayton Christensen with inspiration to the dominant players challenge.

- *Lateral Thinking: Creativity Step by Step* (1970) by Edward de Bono.

- *Harvard Business Review, The Economist, Bloomberg Businessweek, Fortune, The Wall Street Journal,* and *The New York Times*

- *The Practice of Creativity* (1970) by George Prince with insight as to how to enumerate responses and "take your mind on vacation."

- *The Opposable Mind: Winning Through Integrative Thinking* (2009) by Roger Martin

- *The Secret* (2010) by Rhonda Byrne.

- *The Tipping Point: How Little Things Can Make a Big Difference* (2002) by Malcolm Gladwell and the connection to seeing this principle inspire our cultural change at both IBM and PwC.

- *In the Yikes! Zone: A Conversation with Fear* (2002) by Mermer Blakeslee with inspiration to taking innovators risk and learning.

## Companies

- Gillette (now a division of P&G): CFO Chuck Cramb, Robert Murray, and the many senior officers, the learning experiences overseas, and many colleagues while employed at Paper Mate and Toiletries Divisions.

- PepsiCo: many senior officers including CEO Steve Reinemund, Matt McKenna, Fred McRobie, Charlie Rogers, and the learning experiences overseas.

- General Electric: CEOs Jack Welch and Jeff Immelt; many senior officers including Al Cerruti, Dave Calhoun, John Rice; and the learning experiences overseas. I came to know Jack, his management pearls, and GE well over my 10 years as PwC's original Global Client Relationship Leader, and many of Jack's management insights have consciously, and perhaps some unconsciously, seeped into this book.

- Price Waterhouse (PW), PriceWaterhouseCoopers (PwC): nearly 20 years, over 100 Rainmakers, learning opportunities overseas, and the many hundreds of partners I came to know and learn from. And Mark Lutchen and our London partner who helped me see the wisdom in originating our global network.

- Consumer Financial Institute (CFI): Sheldon Laube, Martin Leinwand (my contracting mentor), and the many employees in this entrepreneurial venture.

- IBM: an early customer of CFI, PwC downsizing client, and eventual Rainmaker/leadership mentoring client (after merger).

- Procter & Gamble (P&G): Early CFI Fortune 100 customer, believer, and financial planning proponent.

- NBC Today Show: for early on recognition and inclusion, key staff such as Doreen Jagoda, and over seven hosts including Tom Brokaw and Jane Pauley, Deborah Norville, and others.

- Noxell (division of Gillette): Bob Duke, early on mentor, Peter Troup, lifelong friend and confidant.

- Victory Van Corporation: founded by my father, H. Randolph Barbee in 1945 and run by H. Randolph Barbee, Jr., my brother; now run by Chris Patton, CEO, and David Kennedy, SVP; I am honored to be a 40 year Board member, 1975-Present.

# INDEX

www.InnovationNuggets.com

CPSIA information can be obtained at www.ICGtesting.com
Printed in the USA
BVOW06*2145200616

452745BV00006BA/10/P